Published by Bassline Publishing
www.basslinepublishing.com

ISBN 13: 9798725947304

Notation Legend

The Stave: most music written for the bass guitar uses the bass clef. The example to the right shows the placement of the notes on the stave.

Tablature: this is a graphical representation of the music. Each horizontal line corresponds with a string on the bass guitar, with the lowest line representing the lowest string. The numbers represent the frets to be played. Numbers stacked vertically indicate notes that are played together. Where basses with five or six strings are required, the tablature stave will have five or six lines as necessary.

Notes shown in brackets indicated that a note has been tied over from a previous bar.

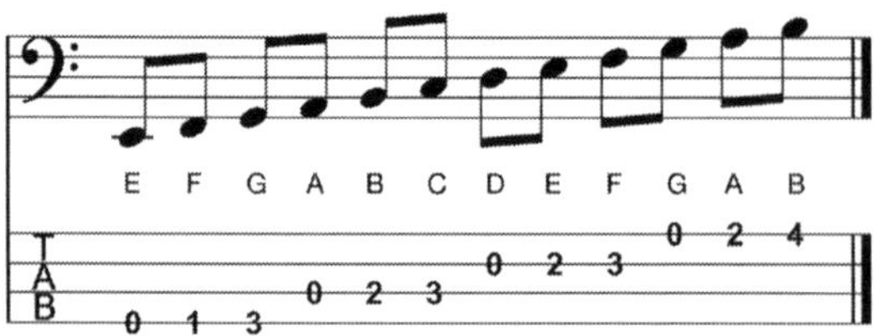

Repeats: the double line and double dot bar lines indicate that the music between these bar lines should be repeated. If the music is to be repeated more than once, a written indication will be given i.e. 'play 3x'.

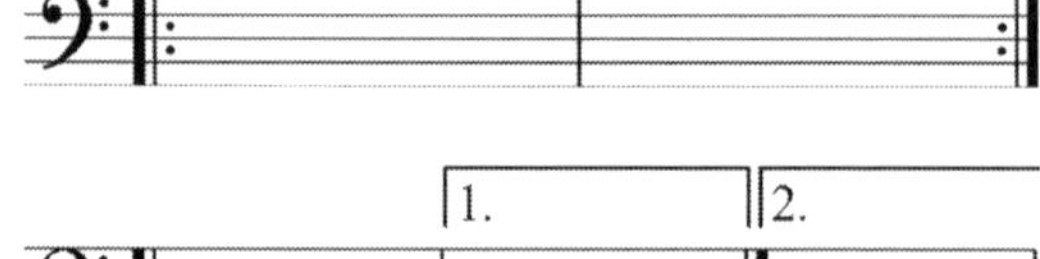

1st & 2nd Time Endings: these are used for sections that are repeated, but which have different endings. The first ending is used the first time, the second is used on the repeat. The first ending is ignored on the repeat, only the second is used.

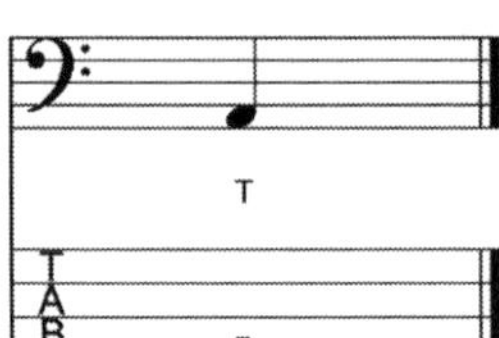

Slap: the note is slapped with the thumb.

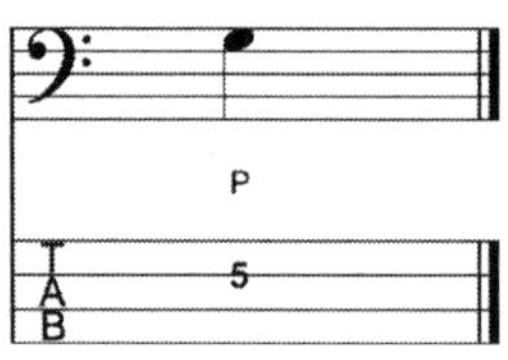

Pop: the note is popped with either the first or second finger.

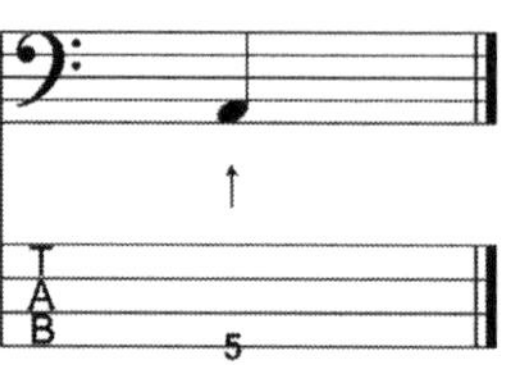

Thumb Up: played with an upstroke of the thumb.

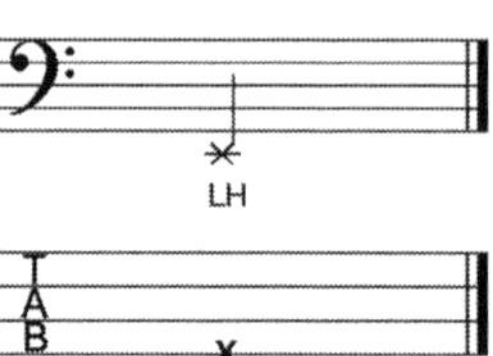

Fretting Hand: played by hammering on with the fretting hand.

Harmonic: note is played as a harmonic by lighting touching the string above the fret indicated.

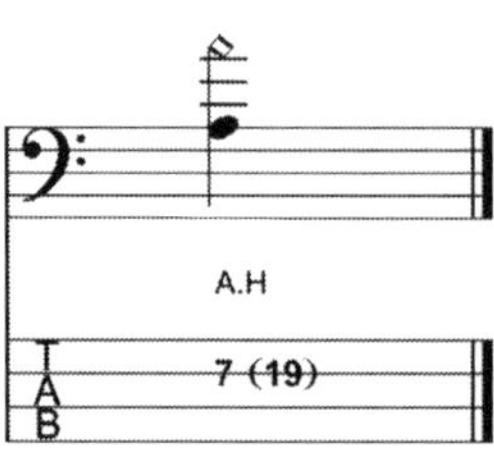

Artificial Harmonic: fret the lower note and tap the string over the fret shown in brackets.

Trill: alternate between the notes indicated by repeatedly hammering-on and pulling-off.

Vibrato: the pitch of the note is altered by repeatedly bending and releasing the string.

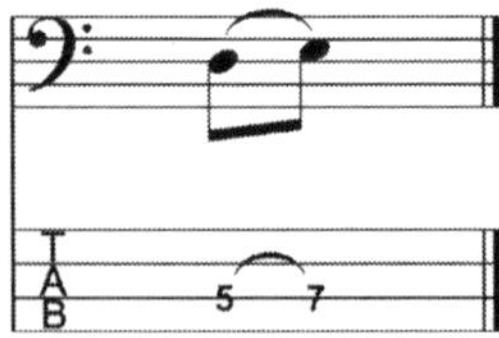

Hammer-On: only the first note is struck. The second is sounded by fretting it with another finger.

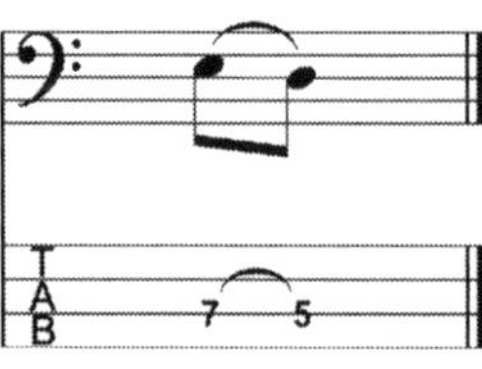

Pull-Off: Only the first note is struck. Lift the fretting finger to sound the second fretted note.

Slide: play the first note, then slide the finger to the second.

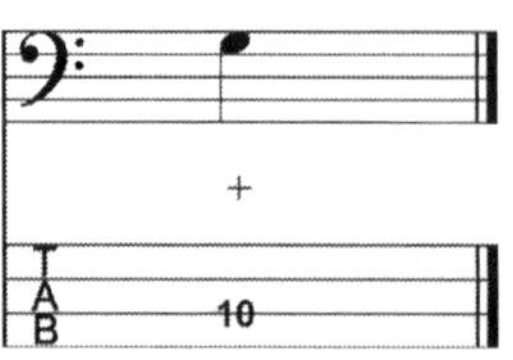

Picking Hand Tap: note is tapped with a finger of the picking hand. If necessary, the finger will be specified.

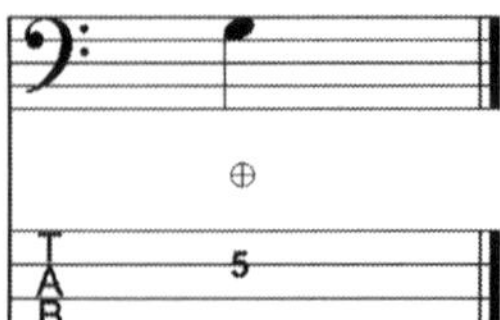

Fretting Hand Tap: note is tapped with a finger of the fretting hand. If necessary, the finger will be specified.

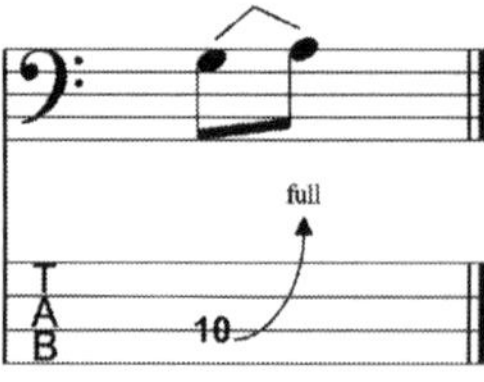

Bend: note is bent upwards to the interval indicated. ½ = half step, full = whole step.

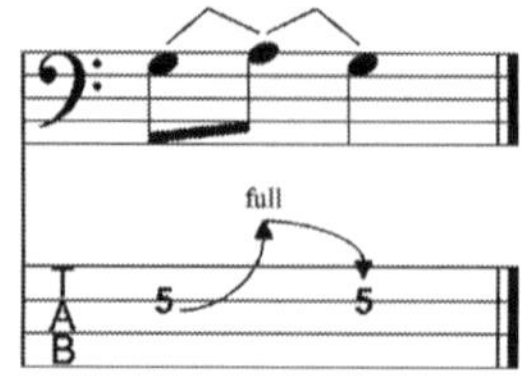

Bend and Release: note is bent up to the interval indicated then released to the original note.

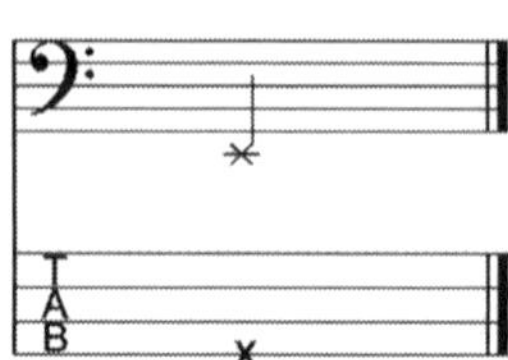

Ghost Note: note is a pitchless 'dead' note used as a rhythmic device.

Accent: note is accentuated, or played louder.

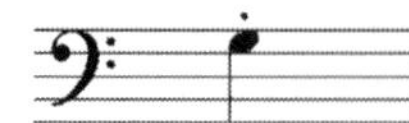

Staccato: note is played staccato - short.

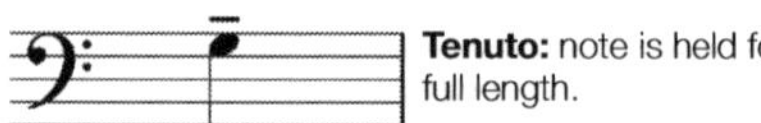

Tenuto: note is held for its full length.

p *piano* - played very softly
mp *mezzo-piano* - played moderately quietly
mf *mezzo forte* - played moderately loud/strong
f *forte* - played loud/strong

D.C al Coda: Return to the beginning of the song and play until the bar marked Coda. Then jump to the section marked Coda.
D.S al Coda: Return to the sign, then play until the bar marked Coda. Then jump to the Coda.
D.C (or D.S) al Fine: Return to the point specified, then play until the Fine marking. Stop at this point.

Contents

Introduction

Welcome to *The Bass Guitarist's Guide to Reading Music: Intermediate Level*, the second in a series of books that will teach you to read music on the bass guitar. This book builds on all of the elements that were introduced in *Beginner Level*, so even if you already have some reading experience, it is recommended that you work through the first volume before starting on this one.

The ability to read music is one of the most important skills to master for an aspiring professional musician. Learning to read fluently will open up many areas of employment that would previously have been unavailable to you – session work, theatre shows, touring and function band work are all examples of paid, professional engagements which require reading musicians. Being able to read also means that you will be able to fill in for other bass players on short notice, as well as write and arrange parts for your own bands – both invaluable skills. Music is a highly competitive industry and in order to succeed in it you should look to find every advantage that you can over your competition. Being the best reader that you can be is an excellent way to do this!

I have written this series of books because after teaching both privately and in music schools for several years I have noticed that there is a distinct lack of material available for bass guitarists who want to learn to read. Many of the books that are available contain predominantly dull, scale-based exercises, with almost no explanation as to *how* you should go about learning to read them. Similarly, very few contain explanations of musical features such as navigation, key signatures, time signatures or dynamics. In this book you'll find that all of these things are covered in detail and are supported by an extensive selection of exercises which will allow you to work on them in a musical way.

Audio Files

This book is also unique in that it includes audio files for all of the exercises. These are available to download free of charge from the Bassline Publishing website. Whilst I believe that it is important to work on reading exercises predominantly with just a metronome, many of my students have raised the valid point: 'how do I know if I'm playing it right?!' The audio files therefore exist as a reference point for you to use to check the accuracy of what you are playing when studying without a teacher present.

To download the audio files, go to www.basslinepublishing.com and log in – if you don't have an account, you'll need to create one. Once logged in, click on FREE Stuff on the main menu. You'll find the audio in a zip file listed under the bonus content for this book.

The majority of the audio consists of bass guitar recorded with only a metronome rather than a full backing track. This has been done to encourage you to learn to keep your place within the score without the safety net of an obvious drum pattern to help you. However, the ten 'real world' exercises at the end of the book are recorded with a full band backing track so that you can put what you have learnt to the test in a more realistic environment. These tracks are available in two forms – with bass and without. You can use the bass tracks for reference if needed, and the backing tracks to play along with.

How to Use This Book

If you have already worked through the first book in this series you will know that in order to be able to read music fluently, you must first understand the language in which it is written. This book aims to continue teaching the fundamentals of that language, building on all of the topics that were covered in the previous one. Again, each new element will be illustrated through the use of examples and exercises.

As before, it's important for you to understand from the beginning that you are not expected to 'sight-read' any of the exercises in this book. Sight reading comes with time and practice, once you have studied the language of music in detail. Instead, these exercises are to be **studied**: when you make a mistake, you should stop and consider what you did wrong: refer to the audio if you need to, or discuss the problem with a teacher. Once you have corrected the mistake, move on. You should keep working through each piece in this manner until you can play it by following the notation. In doing so you will be absorbing the language of written music and learning from the mistakes that you make. The ability to read a piece of music on sight will develop naturally as you follow this path of study.

You should also be aware that the written tempos are merely suggested starting points. These are the tempos that the accompanying audio files were recorded at, but you should not feel that this is where you must start. In fact, you should initially study each exercise in free time, with no metronome putting pressure on you to 'understand quickly'. Once you are comfortable with the notes and rhythms you can begin using the metronome, but don't be afraid to start with tempos that are slower than those that are written.

Finally, whilst this book will help you to take your music reading skills to the next level, it requires two things from you: commitment and lots of hard work! Learning to read music is essentially like learning a new language, albeit a relatively simple one. Doing so will require time, daily practice and patience and although it might be frustrating to begin with, the results will be worth it I can assure you.

I hope that you enjoy this book and that it helps you to become a competent reader. As always, I would be delighted to hear your thoughts, and answer any questions that you might have. Please feel free to send emails to stuart@basslinepublishing.com.

Stuart Clayton
January 2013

Chapter 1

Sixteenth Note Rhythms (Part 1)

This chapter is the first of two that will examine how sixteenth notes are used in music and will demonstrate good approaches to learning to read them. Adding sixteenths into the mix introduces a rhythmic element that will allow us to play a wide range of new rhythms. The scope of the rhythms that are possible using sixteenths can be daunting, so it's essential to approach them in bite-size chunks.

Sixteenth Notes/Semiquavers

Sixteenth notes – also known as **semiquavers** – last for a quarter of a beat in simple time, meaning that four can be played in the space of one quarter note. This in turn means that sixteen sixteenth notes can be played in a bar of 4/4. A single sixteenth note is shown below, as are a group of four beamed together:

You can see that in isolation, a sixteenth note looks similar to an eighth note – it has a black filled note head, a stem and two tails. When sixteenths are beamed together, a double beam is used to represent the two tails.

TIP!

The more tails/beams there are, the faster the notes go by! Eighth notes have only one tail/beam, but sixteenths are twice as fast and therefore have two. Even smaller rhythmic divisions are possible (although these are not frequently used and are beyond the scope of this book); for example thirty-second notes have three tails/beams, and sixty-fourth notes have four!

Counting Sixteenth Notes

Sixteenth notes can be counted as 1-*e*-*&*-*a*-2-*e*-*&*-*a* and so on:

This is an example of a **vocalisation**, a spoken phrase which when said aloud, describes the sound of the rhythm perfectly. Other four syllable words are also used for groups of four sixteenth notes: 'Coca-Cola' and 'Mississippi' are two very common examples that you might have encountered before.

Sixteenth Note Rests

As you can see from the illustration below, the sixteenth note rest is quite similar to the eighth note rest:

Just as sixteenth notes have two tails (or beams), the sixteenth note rest has two tails.

Now that sixteenth notes have been introduced, we have covered the majority of the rhythmic elements that are commonly found in written music. The table below is a recap of all of the rhythms covered so far, each one expressed within a bar of 4/4:

In Use	UK Name	U.S. Name
𝅝	**Semibreve**	**Whole Note**
𝅗𝅥 𝅗𝅥	**Minim**	**Half Note**
♩ ♩ ♩ ♩	**Crotchet**	**Quarter Note**
♫ ♫ ♫ ♫	**Quaver**	**Eighth Note**
♬ ♬ ♬ ♬	**Semiquaver**	**Sixteenth Note**

Combining Eighth Notes and Sixteenth Notes

Sixteenth notes are frequently used in combination with eighth notes and so the focus of this chapter will be to examine three rhythms that are created by combining these two rhythmic values together.

Example 1

The first rhythmic combination is an eighth note followed by two sixteenth notes; essentially a longer note followed by two shorter ones. To count this, try playing a bar of eighths, then splitting the second note of each beat into two shorter notes. You should also listen to the audio file for clarification. In this example, the new rhythm is applied to beats one and three in the first bar, then every beat in the second.

When used on each beat, the result is what is commonly referred to as a 'gallop rhythm'. The reason for this name is more obvious when the rhythm is used at high speeds, since it closely mimics the rhythm of galloping horses. This rhythm was commonly used by early metal bands such as Iron Maiden.

Example 2

The next combination is a reverse of the previous one: two sixteenth notes, followed by an eighth note. To count this rhythm, count eighth notes as before, then split the first of each beat into two quicker notes. Be sure to listen to the relevant audio file as well.

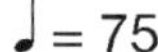

Example 3

The next combination of rhythms is unusual: a sixteenth note, followed by an eighth note, followed by a sixteenth. This rhythm can be awkward to play or sing initially. Listen to the audio file for guidance here.

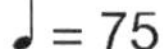

TIP!

A good vocalisation for this rhythm can be heard in the James Brown song 'Get Up (I Feel Like Being a) Sex Machine'. The phrase 'Get on up' is sung in this rhythm and knowing this can be helpful when studying lines that use it.

In addition to these three rhythms, it is also important that you can read and understand variations that incorporate rests. The following three examples all include the eighth note rest.

Example 4

This example is similar to Example 1 but has an eighth note rest followed by two sixteenth notes. If you are comfortable with playing Example 1, you should be able to adapt it by removing the first note of each beat, only playing the two notes that are heard on the upbeat. This rhythm is commonly used by the guitar in reggae music.

♩ = 75

Example 5

This example is the same as Example 2 but has two sixteenth notes followed by an eighth note rest. Again, if you are comfortable playing Example 2, you should be able to easily adapt it accordingly. This rhythm is essentially playing two sixteenth notes, starting on the beat. The second half of each beat is silent.

Example 6

This example is based on the tricky rhythm from Example 3 and is made even more unpleasant with the use of an eighth note rest in the middle! Listen closely to the audio file for guidance with this rhythm.

Rhythm Exercises

The ten exercises that follow are rhythm-only exercises. These are designed to allow you to work on the rhythms covered in this chapter in conjunction with all of the other rhythms that were covered in the previous book.

EXERCISE 1

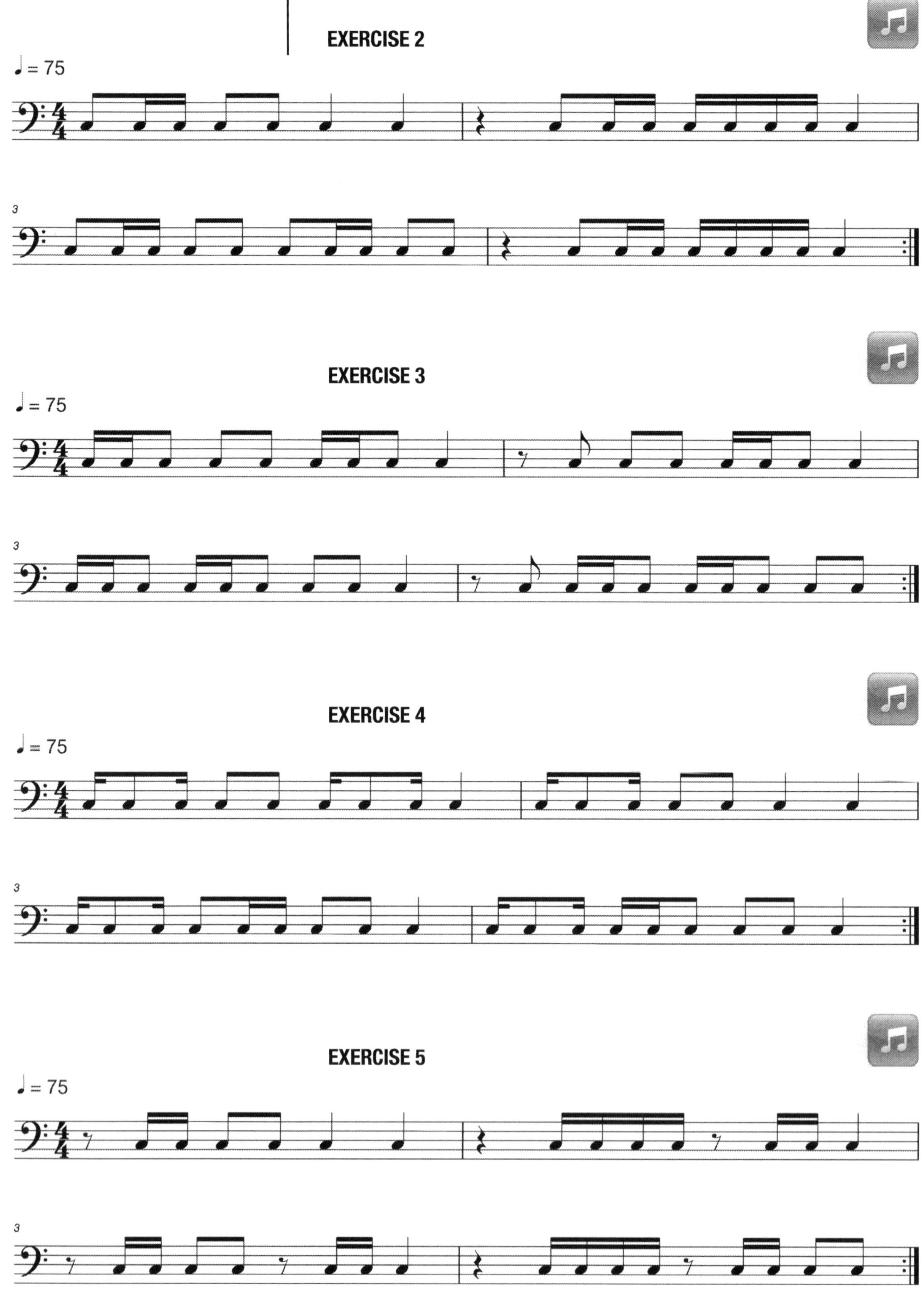
EXERCISE 2
♩= 75
3
EXERCISE 3
♩= 75
3
EXERCISE 4
♩= 75
3
EXERCISE 5
♩= 75
3

EXERCISE 6
♩ = 75
3
EXERCISE 7
♩ = 75
3
EXERCISE 8
♩ = 75
3
EXERCISE 9
♩ = 75
3

EXERCISE 10

Chapter Summary

There has been a lot of new rhythmic information for you to digest in this chapter and I recommend you study it all very carefully, referring to the audio files for guidance where needed. Often, putting rhythms into practice will help reinforce what you see on the page. With that in mind, the following ten exercises will allow you to begin reading basslines that feature these rhythms.

EXERCISE 11

This exercise is a continuous sixteenth note bassline. Although it might look tough, in most bars there is only one note, which is then repeated in the sixteenth note rhythm shown.

♩ = 80

3

5

7

9

11

13

15

EXERCISE 12

This exercise uses the 'gallop rhythm' exclusively. This rhythm is a popular choice for metal songs and bass player Steve Harris has used it in many tracks that he has recorded with his band Iron Maiden. This rhythm is also often used by Mark King of Level 42, notably on the song 'Lessons in Love' which featured an arpeggiated slap bassline using this rhythm.

♩ = 80

EXERCISE 13

This exercise uses the two sixteenths-eighth note rhythm that was demonstrated in Example 2. The second half of the exercise also uses the variation from Example 5: two sixteenth notes followed by an eighth note rest.

♩ = 90

EXERCISE 14

This exercise makes use of the sixteenth-eighth-sixteenth note rhythm from Example 3.

EXERCISE 15

This exercise is a riff-based sixteenth note bassline. The symbol for repeating the previous two bars is also used in this exercise. If you are unsure about this symbol, refer to Chapter 7 in the *Beginner Level* book.

♩ = 80

EXERCISE 16

This exercise again uses the sixteenth-eighth-sixteenth note rhythm, but also features the rhythm used in Example 4: the eighth note rest followed by two sixteenth notes. This rhythm is used at the beginning of each of the first four bars and means that the bass enters on the 'and' of beat one in each bar.

♩ = 80

EXERCISE 17

This exercise uses the rhythms that were introduced in Examples 1 and 2. These are used in different combinations throughout this exercise, so study each bar carefully.

♩ = 80

TIP!

When reading music, even if a bar looks like it is the same as an earlier bar, never assume that it is! There are sometimes some very subtle differences and the best readers will always be able to spot these.

EXERCISE 18

This exercise uses many of the rhythms that were covered in this chapter. As before, be careful not to assume that later bars are repeats of earlier bars – this is not always the case. Look closely!

♩ = 80

EXERCISE 19

This exercise features quite a lot of space. This means that you will have to count beats carefully in order to ensure that the notes are played on the correct beats and the correct *parts* of the beat.

♩ = 80

EXERCISE 20

This exercise looks horrendous to read initially. However, you should quickly notice that the string of eight sixteenth notes is the same in each bar. If you can spot instances of repetition such as this, seemingly difficult exercises suddenly become a lot easier!

♩ = 80

4

7

10

13

Chapter 2
Fifths

This chapter focuses on learning to recognise and read a specific interval – the fifth. This carries from Chapters 5 and 9 from the *Beginner Level* book, in which the intervals of the octave and the third were studied in detail. Fifths, like octaves and thirds are frequently used in basslines from all styles of music, so learning to recognise and play them on the bass is crucial to your development as a reading musician.

You might already be aware that thirds are written on either adjacent lines, or in adjacent spaces, depending on where the root note is located. **Fifths** are similarly recognisable: if the root is in a space, then the fifth will be two spaces above. If the root is on a line, the fifth will be two *lines* above. Here are two examples of fifths:

Fifth in spaces

Fifth on lines

In the second bar of each example the notes are shown stacked vertically to illustrate their appearance on the stave more clearly.

Like thirds, fifths come in two varieties – the **perfect fifth** and the **diminished fifth** (sometimes referred to as a flattened fifth). A perfect fifth is equal to seven half steps (or semitones):

C	C♯	D	D♯	E	F	F♯	G
	1	2	3	4	5	6	7

A diminished fifth is equal to six half steps:

C	C♯	D	D♯	E	F	F♯
	1	2	3	4	5	6

The type of fifth will depend on the key that you are in (remember to look at the key signature!) and whether there are any accidentals in use. Consider the following examples, which are both written in the key of C:

Perfect Fifth

Diminished Fifth

The first example on the previous page is a perfect fifth as C and G are separated by seven half steps. However, the second example is a diminished fifth. Although at first glance you might think that this is another perfect fifth, the interval between B and F is *six* half steps, making a diminished fifth. Every major key contains one diminished fifth interval, starting on the seventh degree of the scale. It's a great idea to bear this in mind when studying the key signature of a piece of music.

TIP!

For more information on fifths (or any other interval for that matter), be sure to check out Chapters 8 & 9 of *The Bass Guitarist's Guide to Scales & Modes*, also available from Bassline Publishing.

It is a good idea to be familiar with the fretboard shape of these two intervals. Both are illustrated below:

Perfect Fifth

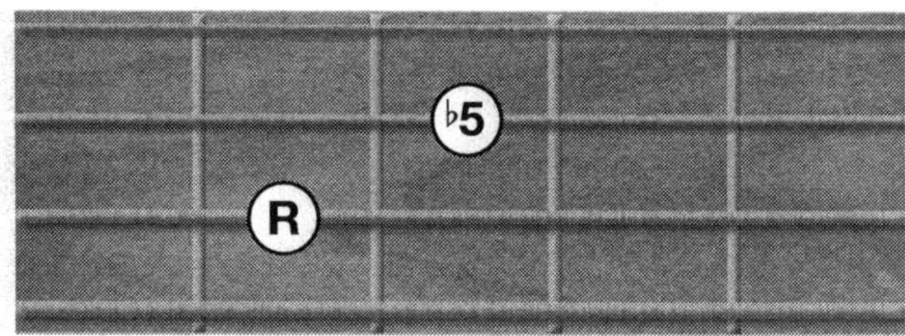

Diminished Fifth

As you can see, the perfect fifth is always on the next string, two frets away. With your first finger on a root note, you'll find that you have easy access to both the perfect fifth and the octave in this hand position. Many basslines are built around this important group of notes, so remembering their locations will make reading them easier.

You'll also be able to see that the diminished fifth is just one fret away, on the next string.

Inverted Fifths

An **inverted fifth** is where the fifth is played *below* the root note rather than above it. If you consider that the fifth of C is G, then you'll probably see quite quickly that it could be played below the root as well as above it. Consider the following example:

Here, the bassline is playing a repeating root-fifth movement between C and G – the root and fifth of the C chord. However, the fifth is used in a lower position than the root – this is a very common root-fifth movement. You will notice that the interval between the root and fifth in this case is actually an intervallic fourth (fourths will be covered in more detail in Chapter 6), but the note is still technically the fifth of C. In the illustration on the next page you can see a root note, the fifth, and the inverted fifth.

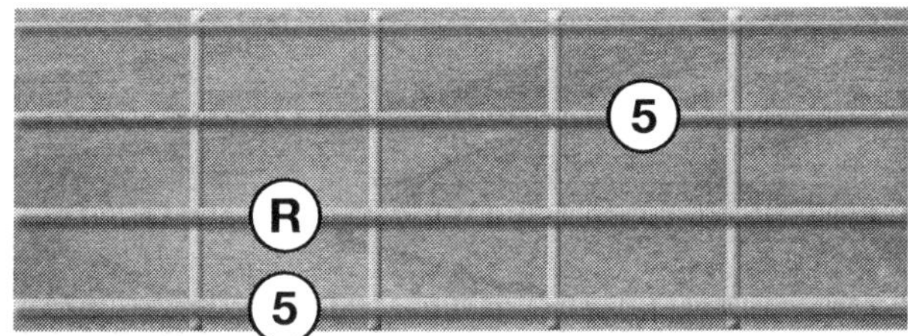

Chapter Summary

This chapter has covered another very important interval – the fifth. Like the third, this is a relatively simple interval to recognise on the stave. The following ten exercises will give you the opportunity to put this to the test. Some of the exercises will also use inverted fifths.

EXERCISE 21

This is a simple rock bassline that uses just root and fifth for each different chord.

♩ = 90

EXERCISE 22

This is a descending minor key bassline based around roots and fifths again. The line is played in a lower octave in the second half of the track.

EXERCISE 23

This is a sixteenth note-based groove that uses fifths extensively.

EXERCISE 24

This exercise uses a root-fifth-octave pattern in bars 5-8. This is a very common bass pattern and you should take time to become familiar with it. In the second half of the exercise the original line is developed slightly and uses the fifth below the root instead of above. The last four bars also feature a root-fifth-ninth idea, which is essentially two fifths played in sequence. For example, B♭-F-C, as seen in bar 13.

EXERCISE 25

This exercise is a slow funk groove in B minor.

EXERCISE 26

This exercise is a rock groove in A minor. This line will also test your ability to read ties.

♩ = 95

EXERCISE 27

This exercise is a slow groove based on the A Phrygian mode, from the key of F major. This line features both the perfect fifth and the diminished fifth intervals.

♩ = 80

EXERCISE 28

This exercise has a Motown flavour to it and uses both fifths and inverted fifths.

EXERCISE 29

This exercise is a root-fifth line which uses a lot of inverted fifths. This kind of line is often used in country music.

EXERCISE 30

This is a simple, ballad-style bassline that makes use of the dotted quarter note-eighth note rhythm that is often used for ballads.

Chapter 3

Dynamics & Articulation

This chapter covers many of the symbols and words that are included in written music, but which have not yet been covered in these books. As you will see, the use of dynamics and articulation makes quite a difference to how music sounds and is performed, so it is therefore important for you to be adept at recognising and understanding all of the words and symbols that are introduced here.

Dynamics

The term **dynamics** is a collective name for written directions that indicate the volume at which music should be played. It also covers other directions and symbols that relate to how it should be performed. Dynamics are abbreviations of Italian words and the two fundamental elements are:

f – an abbreviation of **forte**, the Italian word for strong, or loud.

p – an abbreviation of **piano**, the Italian word for soft.

These directions are then adapted to allow for different degrees of volume:

mf – an abbreviation of **mezzo-forte**, Italian for 'moderately loud'.

mp – an abbreviation of **mezzo-piano**, Italian for 'moderately soft'.

pp – an abbreviation of **pianissimo**, Italian for 'very soft'.

ff – an abbreviation of **fortissimo**, the Italian word for 'very loud'.

More extreme dynamics can be represented by adding additional ***p***'s and ***f***s. For example, ***ppp*** and ***fff*** should leave the reader in no doubt that the piece is to be performed extremely quietly or extremely loud.

In addition to the dynamics covered above, the direction ***sfz*** is sometimes seen. This is a two-part direction: the **s** represents the prefix **subito** which is Italian for 'suddenly'. The ***fz*** translates as **forzando**, the Italian for 'forced'. Therefore, ***sfz*** indicates that the music should suddenly be played loud, or accented. Other ways of accenting notes will be covered later in this chapter.

More gradual changes in volume are represented with **crescendo** and **decrescendo** signs, which are often referred to as 'hairpins' due to their appearance. These are also Italian words, with crescendo meaning 'gradually getting louder' and decrescendo meaning 'gradually getting softer'. Examples of each are shown on the next page.

Example 1 – Crescendo

Example 2 – Decrescendo

In Example 1 the music starts with a direction of ***mp***, meaning moderately soft, and gradually increases in volume to be ***f***, or loud by the end of the second bar. In Example 2, the music starts loud and gradually gets softer, becoming ***p***, or soft, by the end of the second bar.

Performance Directions

Back in Chapter 1 of the *Beginner Level* book it was stated that Italian words often accompany the tempo indication used at the beginning of the piece. As previously mentioned, these are increasingly less common in popular music, but are still used by some musicians and composers, meaning that it is a good idea to be familiar with some of them. Here are some of the more commonly used directions and their translations:

Italian	**Translation**
Meno mosso	Less animated
Più mosso	More animated
A tempo	In time – return to original tempo
Adagio	Slow
Allegretto	Fairly quick
Allegro	Quick
Andante	Medium speed – walking pace
Con moto	With movement
Grave	Very slow, solemn
Largo	Slow
Lento	Slow
Maestoso	Majestically
Moderato	Moderate speed
Presto	Fast
Prestissimo	Very fast
Rubato	Played with freedom
Vivace	Lively, quick
Vivo	Quick

TIP!

If you have a wind-up metronome you might see some of these words written on it next to the corresponding tempos.

More Symbols

There are several other symbols that are commonly used in written music to indicate how individual notes should be performed.

The first of these is the **staccato** dot. This is a dot placed above or below a note head (depending on which way the stem is pointing) and is used to indicate that the note should be played staccato, meaning that it should be played shorter than its actual duration. How much shorter is rather subjective and depends largely on the tempo of the music and the context in which it is used.

TIP!

Be careful not to confuse staccato dots with dots that are written *after* the note. As you know, a dot written after a note extends its rhythmic value by 50%. Staccato dots are always written above or below the note head, NOT after.

The opposite of the staccato dot is the **tenuto** sign. This is a horizontal line written above or below the note head as appropriate. This symbol means that the note should not be shortened in any way and must be held for its full duration.

Finally, individual notes can be accented using the two symbols shown below. The first – typically referred to simply as an **accent** – is the more common by far, although the second – known as **marcato** (Italian for accentuated), is considered a stronger accent.

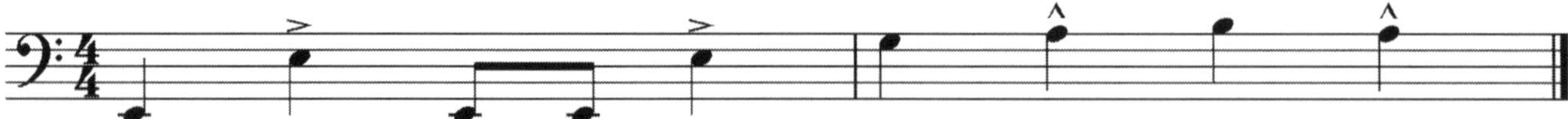

Articulation

Articulation lines are used to indicate that groups of notes are to be played as one unit. The best example of an articulation line is a **slur**, a curved line which is written above two or more notes to indicate that they should be played as one smooth passage, or for vocalists, sung in one breath. Here's an example:

In this example the sixteenth note phrases on beats one and two of each bar are written with a slur above/below them. This indicates that each passage should be played as one smooth, continuous phrase. When used across a string of notes in this way, slurs are often referred to as **phrase marks**.

The more common use of slurs for bass guitarists comes in the form of **hammer-ons, pull-offs, trills** and **shakes**. It's highly likely that you are already familiar with these phrasing tools, but for those who are new to them, an explanation:

Hammer-Ons

A hammer-on is performed by playing a note as normal, then literally 'hammering-on' another note with a different finger further along the same string. Using this technique two or more notes can be sounded after only playing the string once. Here is an example:

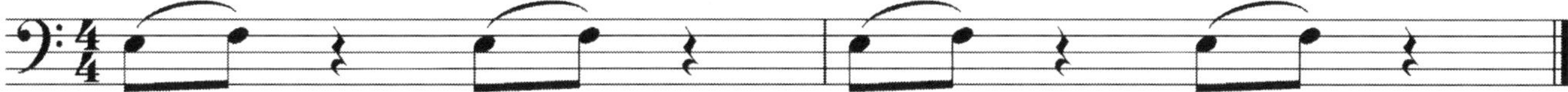

In this example the E is played, then another finger of the fretting hand comes down to sound the F – the string is only played once by the picking hand, but two notes are sounded. As you can see, hammer-ons (which are technically slurs) are shown with a curved line over or below the notes in question to indicate that they are played with one stroke.

Pull-Offs

The opposite of the hammer-on is the pull-off. A pull-off is performed by playing a note, then releasing the finger that is fretting it to sound a note lower on the same string. Here is an example:

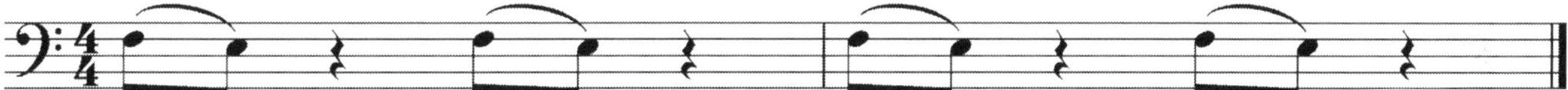

In this example, the F is played with the picking hand, then the finger fretting it lifts up to allow the E on the fret below to sound. In order for this to work, the E must also be fretted before the pull-off is performed.

TIP!

Do not confuse hammer-ons or pull-offs with ties! They look very similar but have very different meanings. Remember that ties are used to connect two identical notes whereas slurs are used to indicate different notes that are played with one stroke.

Trills

A **trill** is a decoration that is a combination of hammer-ons and pull-offs played in very rapid succession. Again, only the first note is struck, and the rest of the notes are created by hammering-on and pulling-off quickly. A trill is indicated by the letters **tr** over a note, followed by a wavy line. The first note of the trill is written as normal, with the second shown smaller and in brackets. A trill lasts for the duration of the note it is written over. Here is an example:

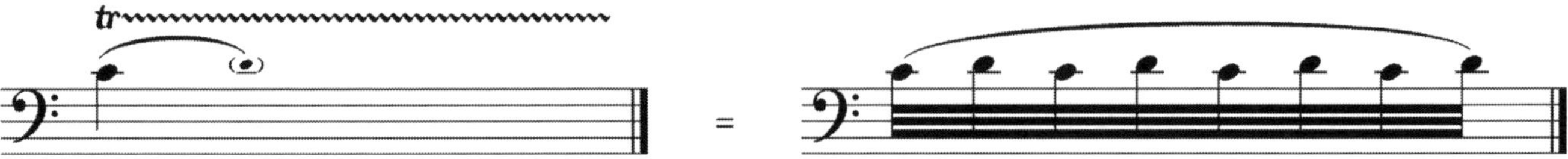

Note that although a trill contains many iterations of the two notes (as shown in the second bar above), only one of each is written. How many of each are played is left to the individual, who would typically alternate between them as quickly as possible.

Shakes

Shakes are similar to trills but are played in a different way: to play a shake, the same finger of the fretting hand is used to slide very rapidly back and forth between two notes, which on the bass guitar, are often a half step apart. Shakes are indicated as follows:

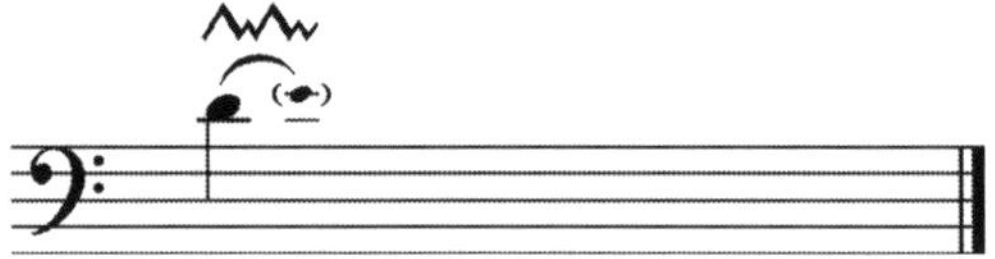

Slides

Slides – also known as **glissandos** – are also examples of slurs. You may see a slanted line connecting two notes as well as the curved line over them. This means that you should slide the fretting finger from one note to the next, only plucking the first note. Here is an example of a slide:

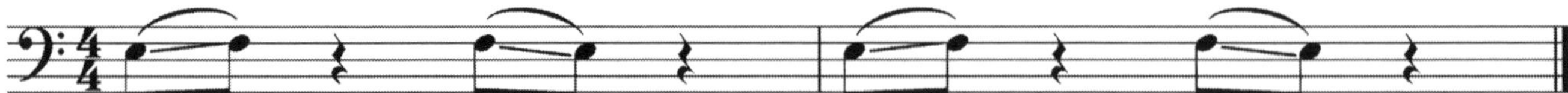

Slides can also be played from a single note, and this is common in music written for the bass guitar. In the example shown below, the note is played, then the finger fretting it slides down the string quickly, away from the note:

Vibrato

Vibrato is a rapid variation in the pitch of a note, played by quickly moving the fretting finger up and down. Vibrato is notated with a wavy line over the note:

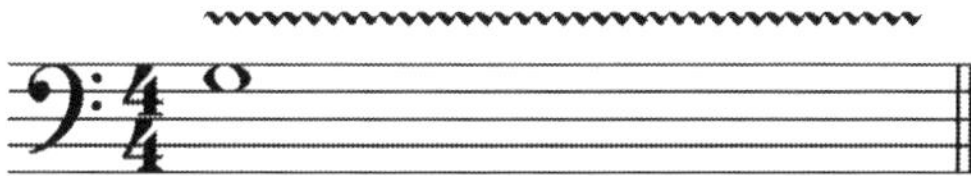

The method most commonly used by guitarists and bassists is to move the string vertically. To do this, simply play a note, then move the string up and down slightly with the finger that is fretting it – you will hear the note 'wobble.' The other way to play vibrato is to shake your finger from side to side on the string. This method stems from the world of classical music and is used by violinists and other members of the string section. This method is more effective on a fretless bass than a fretted.

Ghost Notes

Many styles of bass playing feature the use of **ghost notes** which are pitch-less 'dead' notes that are used for percussive effect. Ghost notes are very commonly used in slap bass grooves, as well as fingerstyle funk grooves. Ghost notes are written on the stave with a cross note head as shown below:

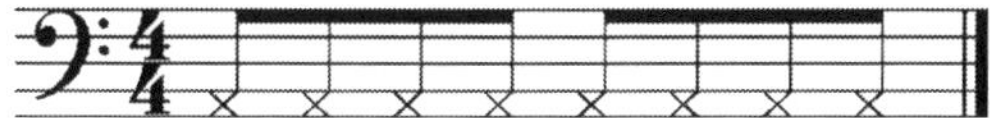

Ghost notes can be played anywhere on the bass but are commonly written on the string that is most convenient to play them on. In the example above they are written in the 'A' space, so would be best played on the A-string.

Chapter Summary

This chapter has introduced many new symbols and words for you to remember, all of which will be used in many of the exercises in the remaining part of the book. When studying an exercise, you should refer back to this chapter if you are unsure what a particular word or symbol means.

Chapter 4

More Key Signatures

This chapter is a continuation of Chapter 11 from the previous book, in which key signatures were introduced. So far, only key signatures with up to two sharps/flats have been used – this chapter will introduce the keys that use three and four sharps/flats.

Sharp Keys

The first key that will be covered here is the key of A major, which has a key signature of three sharps. The two sharps that were in the key of D major remain in place (F♯ and C♯), and a new sharp is added: G♯. Hopefully you'll recall that the new sharp that is added every time is the **leading note**, or major seventh of the new key.

A Major Scale

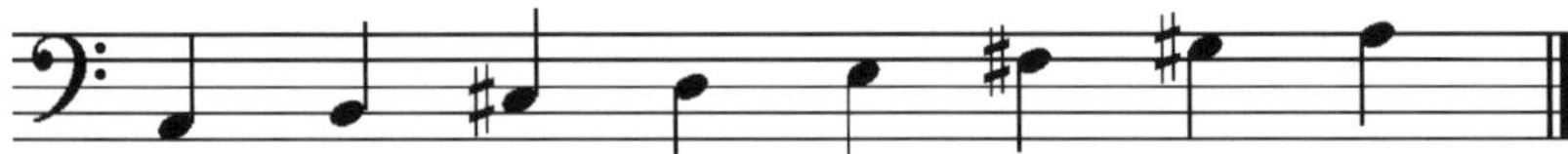

A Major Key Signature

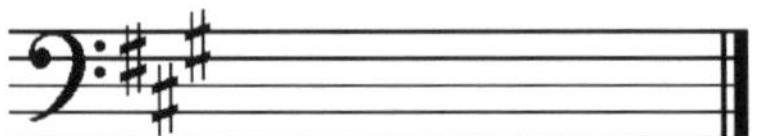

> **TIP!**
>
> When you see a key signature that uses sharps, you can easily figure out the key by looking at the last sharp that is written, and then counting up a half step from there. For example, a key signature of two sharps has C♯ as the last sharp written. Count up one half step and you have a D, which is the key.

Remember that every key signature applies to both a major key, and the relative minor key. Once you know the major key, you can count up six scale degrees to find the relative minor. In the case of A major, the relative minor key is F♯ minor:

A	B	C♯	D	E	F♯	G♯	A
1	2	3	4	5	6	7	8

The next sharp key is E major, which has four sharps. The three sharps from the previous key of A major remain (F♯, C♯ and G♯) and a new sharp is added: D♯. Remember that the new sharp is always the leading note of the new key.

E Major Scale

E Major Key Signature

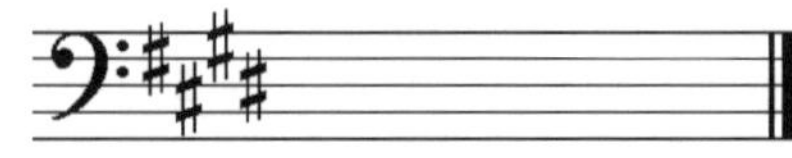

Counting up through the E major scale six degrees will reveal that the relative minor key is C♯ minor.

TIP!

For more on keys and key signatures, be sure to check out *The Bass Guitarist's Guide to Scales & Modes*, also available from Bassline Publishing.

Flat Keys

The next flat key signature has three flats and is the key signature for E♭ major. As you'll be aware if you have studied the previous book, to work out the key from a flat key signature, simply look at the second to last flat that is written. Whatever flat that is, is also the key. For example, a key signature with two flats has B♭ as its second to last flat (in this instance it's also the first flat written). This tells us that the key is B♭ major. Similarly, a key with three flats has E♭ as its second to last flat – this tells us that the key is E♭.

E♭ Major Scale

E♭ Major Key Signature

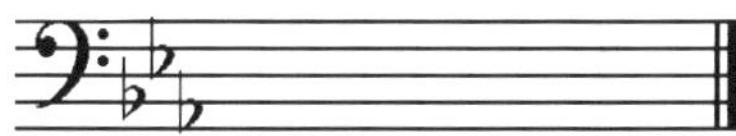

Counting up six degrees through the E♭ major scale will show you that the relative minor key of E♭ major is C minor.

The next flat key is the key of A♭ major, which has four flats. All of the existing flats remain (B♭, E♭, and A♭) and a new one is added – D♭. The second to last flat of the new key signature (A♭) tells us the name of the key.

A♭ Major Scale

A♭ Major Key Signature

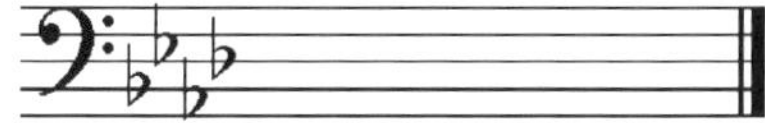

Again, counting up through the A♭ major scale six degrees will show you that the relative minor key is F minor.

As you now know, a key signature tells you that the music is written in either a major key, or the relative minor key. Figuring out which it is means looking at the chord progression, or the notes that are played. For example, if the key signature has three flats, the piece will be written in either E♭ major or C minor. If the first chord is C minor, then this is a good indication that the piece is written in C minor. You can draw the same conclusions by looking at the notes used in the bassline: if the part is based around C, then it is likely that the key is C minor.

Chapter Summary

This chapter has introduced you to eight new keys to play in: A major, E major, E♭ major, A♭ major, and their respective relative minor keys. The ten exercises that follow will allow you to practice reading music that is written in these keys. Although more sharps and flats have now been added, remember that you can easily discern the key by raising the last sharp a half step, or by looking at the second to last flat written.

EXERCISE 31

This exercise has a key signature of three flats, meaning that it is either in the key of E♭ major or C minor. As the bassline starts on – and is centred around E♭ – the key is therefore E♭ major.

♩ = 85

EXERCISE 32

This exercise is in the key of A major.

♩ = 85

EXERCISE 33

This exercise is in the key of E major.

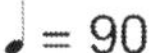

EXERCISE 34

This exercise is in the key of A♭ major.

EXERCISE 35

This exercise has a key signature of three sharps, but this time is in the key of F♯ minor – the relative minor of A major.

EXERCISE 36

This exercise has a key signature of three flats and is in the key of C minor, the relative minor key of E♭ major.

EXERCISE 37

This exercise has a key signature with four sharps and is in the key of C♯ minor, the relative minor key of E major.

♩ = 90

f

EXERCISE 38

This exercise has a key signature of four flats and is in the key of F minor, the relative minor of A♭ major.

♩ = 85

mf

EXERCISE 39

This exercise has a key signature of three sharps and is in the key of F♯ minor, the relative minor key of A major.

♩ = 90

EXERCISE 40

This exercise has a key signature of three flats and is in the key of C minor, the relative minor key of E♭ major.

♩ = 90

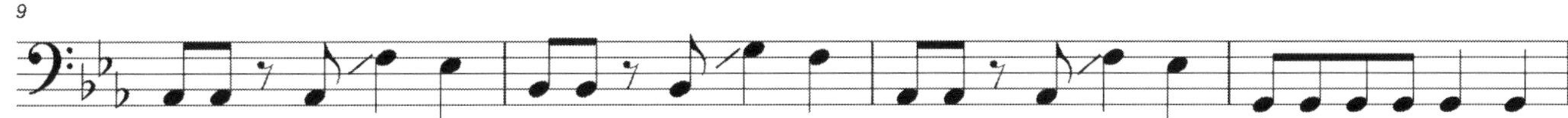

Chapter 5

Sixteenth Note Rhythms (Part 2)

This chapter is the second of three to cover the use of sixteenth notes in music and demonstrates some logical approaches to reading more complex rhythms. As you will have seen from Chapter 1, sixteenth notes allow for a much wider range of rhythmic possibilities, more of which are covered here. This chapter focuses predominantly on the use of sixteenth note rests.

Using Sixteenth Note Rests

As you already know, a quarter note beat can be divided into four sixteenth note **subdivisions**. A sixteenth note rest can be used in any of these subdivisions, creating different rhythms. The first four examples will examine the effect of using a rest on each different subdivision of the beat.

Example 1

In this example, a sixteenth note rest is used in the first subdivision, at the beginning of the beat. This is followed by three sixteenth notes, which complete the beat. There is a rest on beat two (to give your brain time to absorb this rhythm), then the new rhythm is repeated on beat three. Listen to the audio file for this example and try playing along – you might like to think of playing this and using a vocalisation such as 'Co-ca-Co-la' or '1-e-&-a', but not playing on the first syllable.

Example 2

In this example there is a sixteenth note rest on the second subdivision of the beat. The first note is played on the beat and the next two notes start on the upbeat.

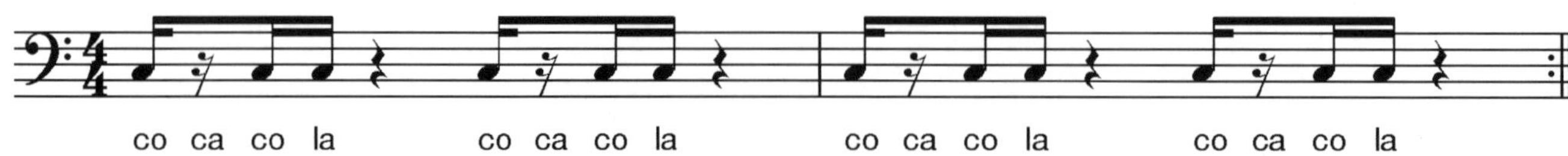

As you might be able to hear, this rhythm is essentially identical to the eighth-two sixteenths 'gallop' rhythm that was introduced in Chapter 1 – the notes are played in the same subdivisions. The only difference is that as the first note is a sixteenth note in this example, it is played as a shorter note. Therefore, this rhythm could alternatively be written in as illustrated below: using an eighth note marked staccato. You are likely to encounter both methods in written music.

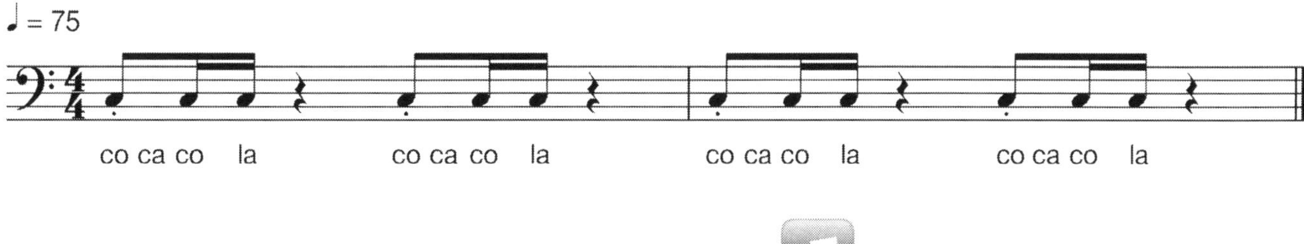

Example 3

In this example, the rest is on the third subdivision of the beat. This means that two notes are played in quick succession starting on the beat and are followed by a third note on the last subdivision of the beat – essentially just before the next beat.

This rhythm is therefore similar to the sixteenth-eighth-sixteenth rhythm from Chapter 1 – the notes are played in the same subdivisions, but the use of the rest makes the second note shorter. As you can see from the example below, this rhythm could also be written by using a staccato dot on the eighth note in the middle of the rhythm:

Again, both are commonly used.

Example 4

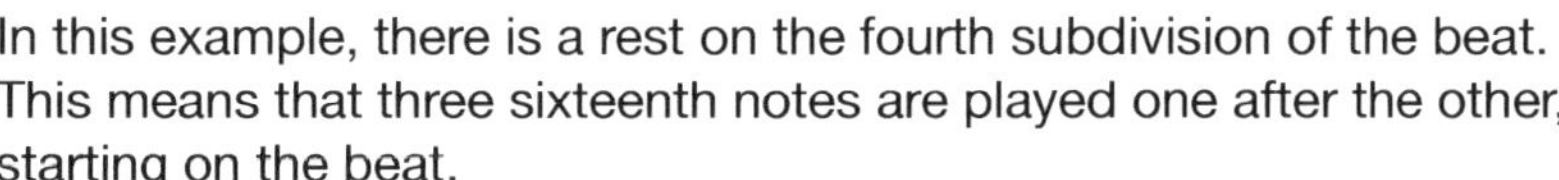

In this example, there is a rest on the fourth subdivision of the beat. This means that three sixteenth notes are played one after the other, starting on the beat.

This rhythm is therefore the same in terms of note placement as the two sixteenths-eighth note rhythm from Chapter 1. The notes are played on the same subdivisions of the beat, but as the last note is a sixteenth, it is a shorter note. As you can see from the example below, this rhythm could also be written with a staccato dot on the eighth note.

♩ = 75

Of course, sometimes more than one sixteenth note rest will be used within the space of a beat. The next two examples illustrate the ways in which this might happen.

Example 5

In this example, the beat starts with a sixteenth note rest, is followed by a sixteenth note, another rest, and a final sixteenth note. This is a heavily syncopated sixteenth note rhythm and is about as bad as reading rhythms ever gets!

♩ = 75

This can be a challenging rhythm to read, so I would offer the following advice: first, listen carefully to the audio file to give yourself an idea of how this rhythm sounds. You should also try playing along with the track. Next, try playing a very quiet ghost note **on** the beat, just before the first sixteenth note:

♩ = 75

Playing a quiet downbeat note makes it a lot easier to place the note on the second subdivision of the beat, since it will come directly after the ghost note. You should then play the next note thinking of it falling *just before* the next beat, or just before you tap your foot for beat two.

Example 6

In this example a sixteenth note rest is used at either end of a beat, with the middle two subdivisions containing notes.

♩ = 75

Again, you might find this rhythm easier to play by adding a quiet ghost note to the downbeat. After doing so, both notes will be played in quick succession – you will essentially be playing three sixteenth notes one after the other, starting on the beat with a ghost note. This is basically the same as the rhythm in Example 4.

Sometimes only one sixteenth note will be played, and the remainder of the beat will be silent. The next four examples will illustrate each of the possible permutations of this.

Example 7

In this example, one sixteenth note is played on the first subdivision of the beat. As this note falls on the beat, this is easy to do: simply play a note on the beat and keep it short.

Note that a dotted eighth note rest has been used here to complete the beat – these have not been seen in the book so far. As you know, adding a dot to a rhythm increases its value by 50%. Therefore, the dotted eighth note rest lasts for three quarters of a beat. Dotted eighth notes and their rests will be covered in the next book in this series.

Example 8

In this example the sixteenth note is played on the second subdivision of the beat. This can be quite a tricky rhythm to understand, but it often helps to think of the note falling *just after* the downbeat. Listen to the audio file and tap your foot on the beat. You should hear that the note falls just after the downbeat.

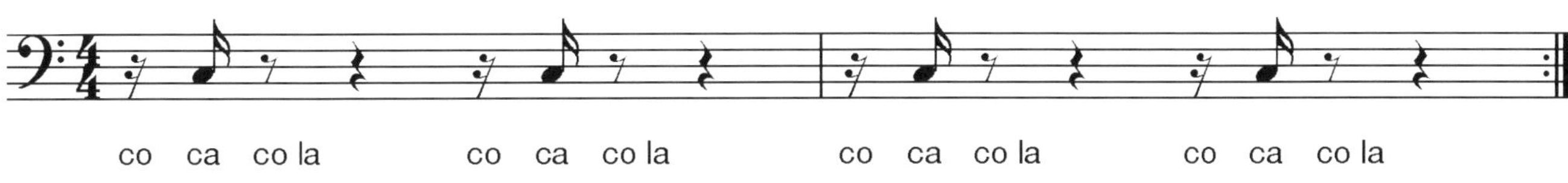

Example 9

In this example the sixteenth note is played on the third subdivision of the beat. This is essentially the same as playing a note on the offbeat, just as you did with eighths in the *Beginner Level* book. The only difference is that since this note is a sixteenth, it should be played as a shorter note.

♩ = 75

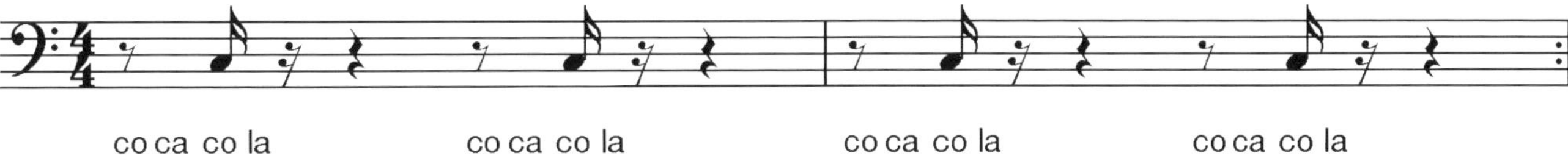

Example 10

In this example the sixteenth note is played on the fourth and final subdivision of the beat. This means that the note is played at the very end of the beat, but you might find it easier to 'feel' this note as falling *just before* the next beat. Listen to the audio file and tap your foot along to the click. As you play the note, you will hear that it falls just before the next beat, leading into it.

Example 11

This is an exercise based on the four examples above. In each of the first four bars, a sixteenth note is played on each of the different subdivisions of the beat. In the next four bars, the same thing happens, but within the second beat of the bar. This encourages you to count the beats in the bar as well as consider which subdivision to play the note in! The next time through the notes are played within the third beat, and then within the fourth beat. Good luck with this exercise – it's tough, but if you can get it together you will have greatly enhanced your understanding of sixteenth notes and subdivisions.

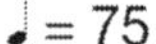

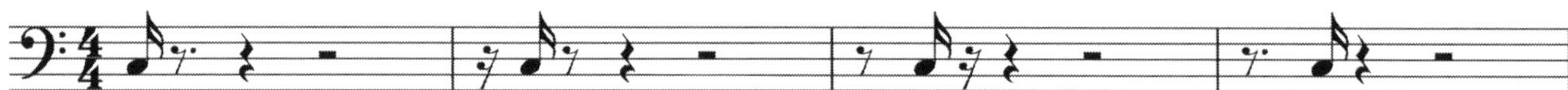

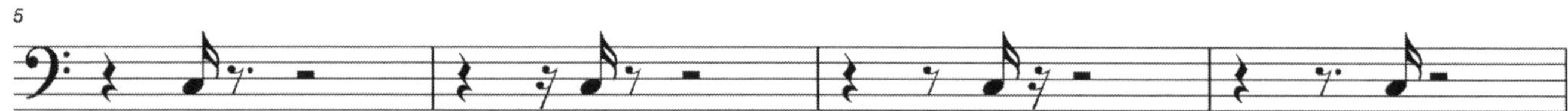

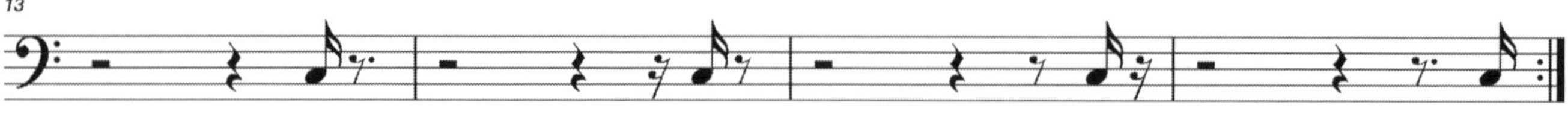

Rhythm Exercises

The following ten exercises are rhythm-only exercises that will allow you to practice reading the rhythms that have been covered in this chapter. These will be combined with all of the rhythms that have been covered so far.

EXERCISE 44
♩ = 75
3
EXERCISE 45
♩ = 75
3
EXERCISE 46
♩ = 75
3
EXERCISE 47
♩ = 75
3

EXERCISE 48

♩ = 75

EXERCISE 49

♩ = 75

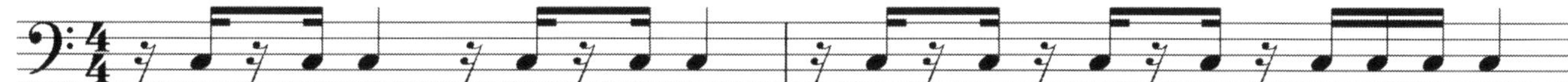

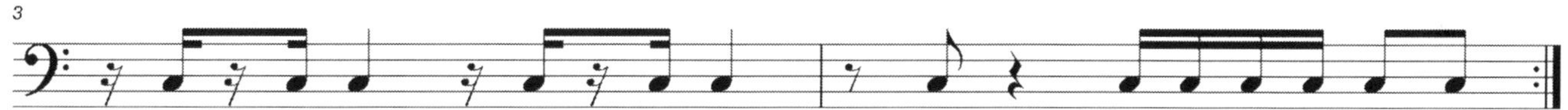

EXERCISE 50

♩ = 75

Chapter Summary

This chapter has demonstrated several further rhythmic permutations involving sixteenth notes and sixteenth note rests. You should now review all of these carefully in conjunction with the audio files and move on to the next group of exercises only when you are confident that you understand them fully.

The next ten exercises will demonstrate all of the new sixteenth note rhythms from this chapter in the context of actual music, which should enhance your understanding of these new rhythms. Be aware that these exercises are in many cases very difficult! Using sixteenth notes and their corresponding rests adds a whole new layer of complexity to music and it is therefore essential that you study these exercises slowly and carefully. Once again, I must stress that you are not expected to sight read these exercises, but to learn them from the notation. Sight reading complex rhythms such as these comes with years of experience!

EXERCISE 51

This exercise features the rhythm from Example 1: a sixteenth note rest, followed by three sixteenth notes.

♩ = 80

mf

EXERCISE 52

This exercise uses the displaced sixteenth note rhythm from Example 8. On beats one and two of most bars, the note is played on the second sixteenth note subdivision (just after the downbeat).

♩ = 80

EXERCISE 53

This exercise will allow you to focus on the difference between two very similar rhythms: the eighth-two sixteenths rhythm that was covered back in Chapter 1 and the rhythm that was demonstrated in Example 2 of this chapter. This rhythm is essentially the same as the first, but as the first note is a sixteenth note instead of an eighth note, it is shorter.

♩ = 80

mf

4

7

11

14

EXERCISE 54

This exercise features the displaced sixteenth note rhythm that was demonstrated in Example 10. When playing this exercise, the first note is played just before the downbeat of beat two.

EXERCISE 55

This is another exercise which uses the rhythm from Example 1 – a sixteenth note rest, followed by three sixteenth notes.

♩ = 85

mf

4

7

10

13

15

EXERCISE 56

This exercise features several of the rhythms covered in this chapter and although it looks complex on paper, you will find that the majority of the exercise is based on the idea from the first two bars.

♩ = 85

mf

4

7

10

13

15

EXERCISE 57

This exercise will allow you to focus on the heavily syncopated rhythm that was demonstrated in Example 5.

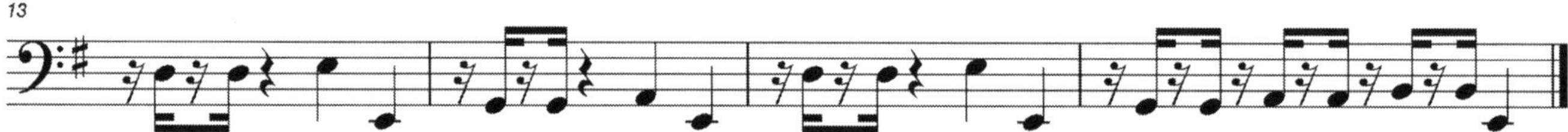

EXERCISE 58

This exercise uses the rhythm that was covered in Example 6. This rhythm can look confusing on paper when used on sequential beats, as it is in bar 4 – the sixteenth note rests at the beginning and the end of each beat can make it difficult to distinguish between the beats. When studying exercises such as this one you might find it useful to draw pencil lines between each beat so that you can clearly see which beat the rests belong to.

♩ = 85

mf

EXERCISE 59

This exercise features a lot of space and will allow you to work on several of the rhythms covered in this chapter.

EXERCISE 60

This exercise also features many of the rhythms covered in this chapter and looks worse on paper than it is to play. Be careful of the subtle differences to the rhythm in bars 13 and 15 in comparison to bars 5 and 7.

♩ = 80

mf

4

8

12

15

Chapter 6

Fourths

This chapter examines the interval of the fourth in detail. This is another important interval and the ability to recognise it on the stave will be a great help to you as you continue to study written music.

As this is the fourth chapter to focus on a specific interval, you should now have a good idea of the benefits of understanding how an interval sounds, as well as how it looks on the stave. Unfortunately, fourths are not quite as simple to recognise on the stave as thirds and fifths were. Whereas thirds exist in adjacent lines and spaces and fifths are separated by a line or a space, fourths are somewhere in between. Two examples of fourths are shown in the examples below:

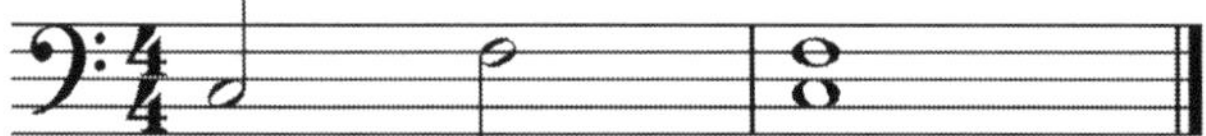

Fourth with root in a space

Fourth with root on a line

In the second bar of each example the notes are shown stacked vertically to illustrate their appearance on the stave more clearly. As you can see, if the root note is written in a space, the fourth above is written two lines up. If the root note is written on a line, the fourth above is written two *spaces* up.

Like thirds and fifths, there are two types of fourth: the **perfect fourth** and the **augmented fourth** (sometimes referred to as a sharpened fourth). A perfect fourth is equal to five half steps (semitones):

C	**C♯**	**D**	**D♯**	**E**	**F**
	1	2	3	4	5

An augmented fourth is equal to six half steps:

C	**C♯**	**D**	**D♯**	**E**	**F**	**F♯**
	1	2	3	4	5	6

TIP!

You might recall from the previous book that the interval of a diminished fifth was also equal to six half steps. This is because both the augmented fourth and the diminished fifth point to the same notes. For example, C-G♭ is a diminished fifth, while C-F♯ is an augmented fourth. G♭ and F♯ are the same note and are referred to as being 'enharmonically equivalent'.

The type of fourth will depend on the key that you are in (remember to look at the key signature!) and whether there are any accidentals in use. Consider the following example, which is written in the key of C:

Perfect Fourth

Augmented Fourth

The first example is a perfect fourth as C and F are separated by five half steps. However, the second example is an *augmented* fourth. Although at first glance it also looks like a perfect fourth, the interval between F and B is six half steps, making it an augmented fourth.

Every major key contains one augmented fourth interval, starting on the fourth degree of the scale. It's a great idea to bear this in mind when studying the key signature of a piece of music.

TIP!

For more information on fourths (or any other interval for that matter), be sure to check out Chapters 8 & 9 of *The Bass Guitarist's Guide to Scales & Modes*, also available from Bassline Publishing.

It is a good idea to be familiar with the fretboard shape of these two intervals. Both are illustrated below:

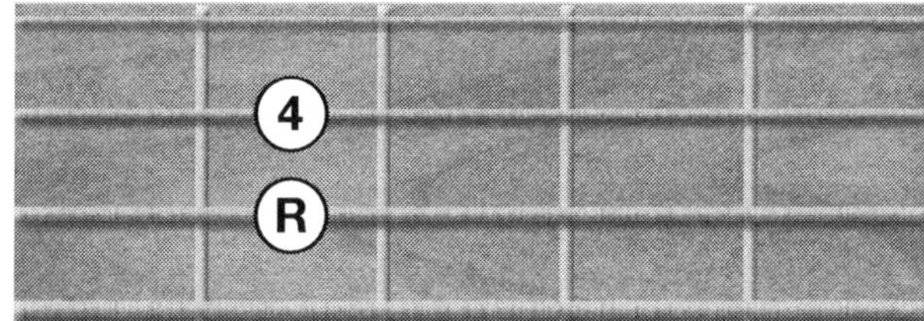

Perfect Fourth

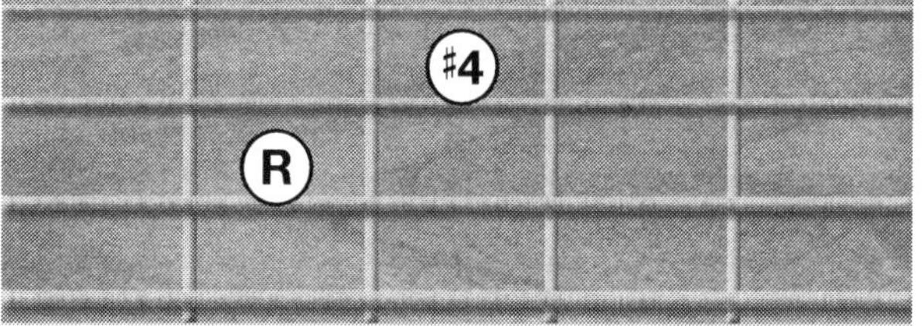

Augmented Fourth

As you can see, the perfect fourth is always on the next string, on the same fret. With your first finger on a root note, you'll find that you have easy access to the perfect fourth by barring across to the next string with the same finger. Many basslines are built around the interval of the perfect fourth, so knowing its location on the fingerboard will make reading them easier.

You'll also be able to see that the augmented fourth is one fret away, on the next string. This is exactly the same location as the **diminished fifth**, which as stated earlier, is the enharmonic equivalent.

Chapter Summary

This chapter has covered another important interval – the fourth. This interval is not quite so easy to recognise on the stave as the third and fifth, although after studying the following ten exercises, you should be quite familiar with it.

EXERCISE 61

This exercise is a simple rock-funk idea. In the first bar, the bassline begins on A, then moves up a fourth to D. This is then repeated a tone lower in the second bar. These bars are followed by two bars of syncopated parts based around the low E. These four bars then form the basis for the rest of the line.

EXERCISE 62

This exercise is a sixteenth note-based groove that makes repeated use of the fourth interval throughout.

♩ = 90

mf

EXERCISE 63

This is a simple rock bassline that is reminiscent of the classic Nirvana song 'Smells Like Teen Spirit'.

EXERCISE 64

This is a rock riff which uses the interval of a fourth extensively.

♩ = 95

mf

EXERCISE 65

This exercise is a funk bassline that uses a repeating figure based on fourths in each bar.

♩ = 90

mf

4

7

10

13

15

EXERCISE 66

This line uses an idea based on fourths as the main motif in each bar.

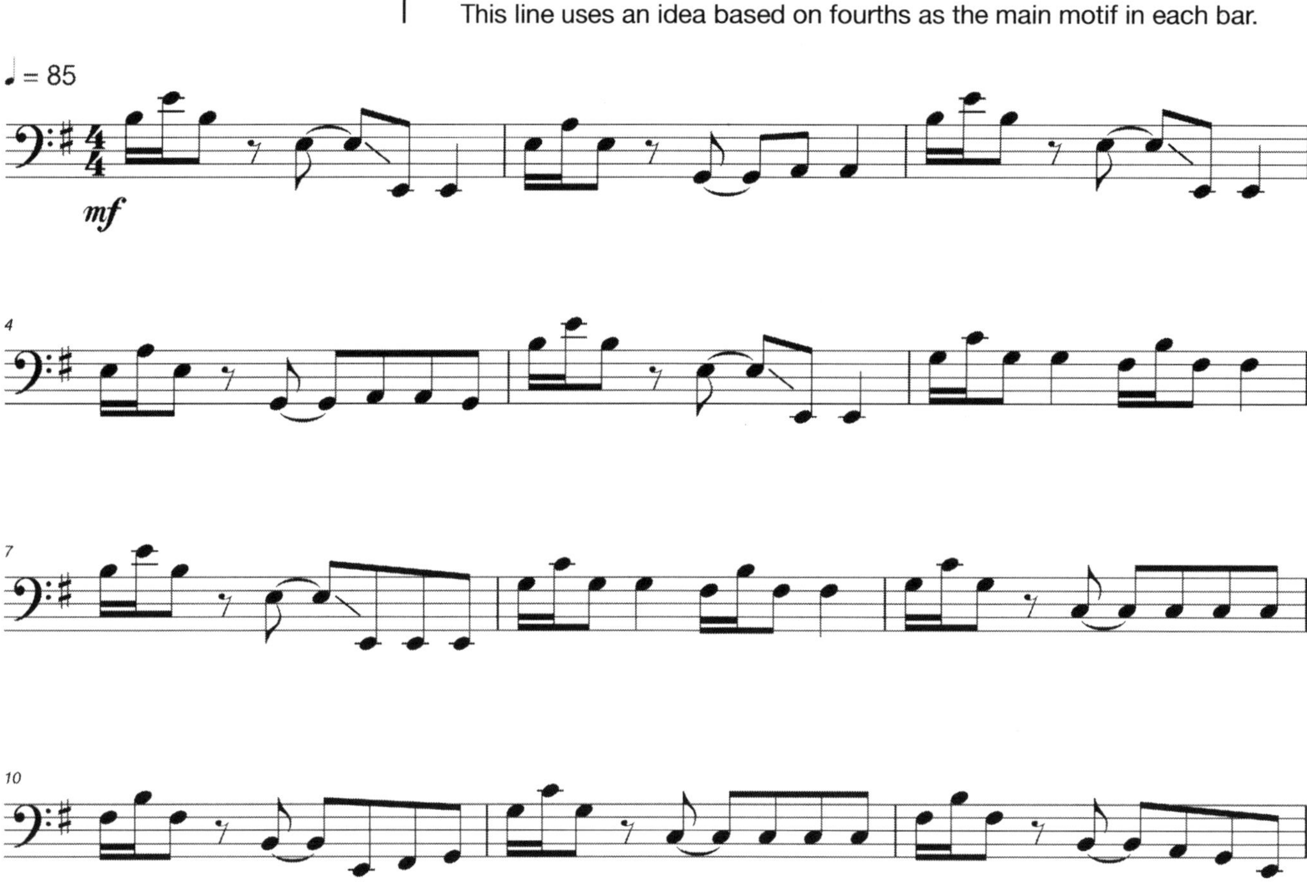

EXERCISE 67

This exercise is a funk bassline that opens with an obvious motif using a fourth. The various fills used throughout the piece also make extensive use of this interval.

EXERCISE 68

This exercise might look unpleasant, but it has a slow tempo and there is a lot of repetition. The fourth interval that is used frequently throughout (the first two notes for example) starts from the fifth in a fifth-octave movement for each of the implied chords.

TIP!

This exercise starts with a one note 'pick-up' just before the first bar. This pick-up is known as an 'anacrusis' and can be any combination of rhythms that is less that a bar long.

EXERCISE 69

The main section of this exercise features two fourths in the first part of the bar. This is then followed by some root note-based riffing. The middle section of the piece (bars 9-12) features a chromatically descending line where each root note is approached by the fifth, which is an intervallic fourth below.

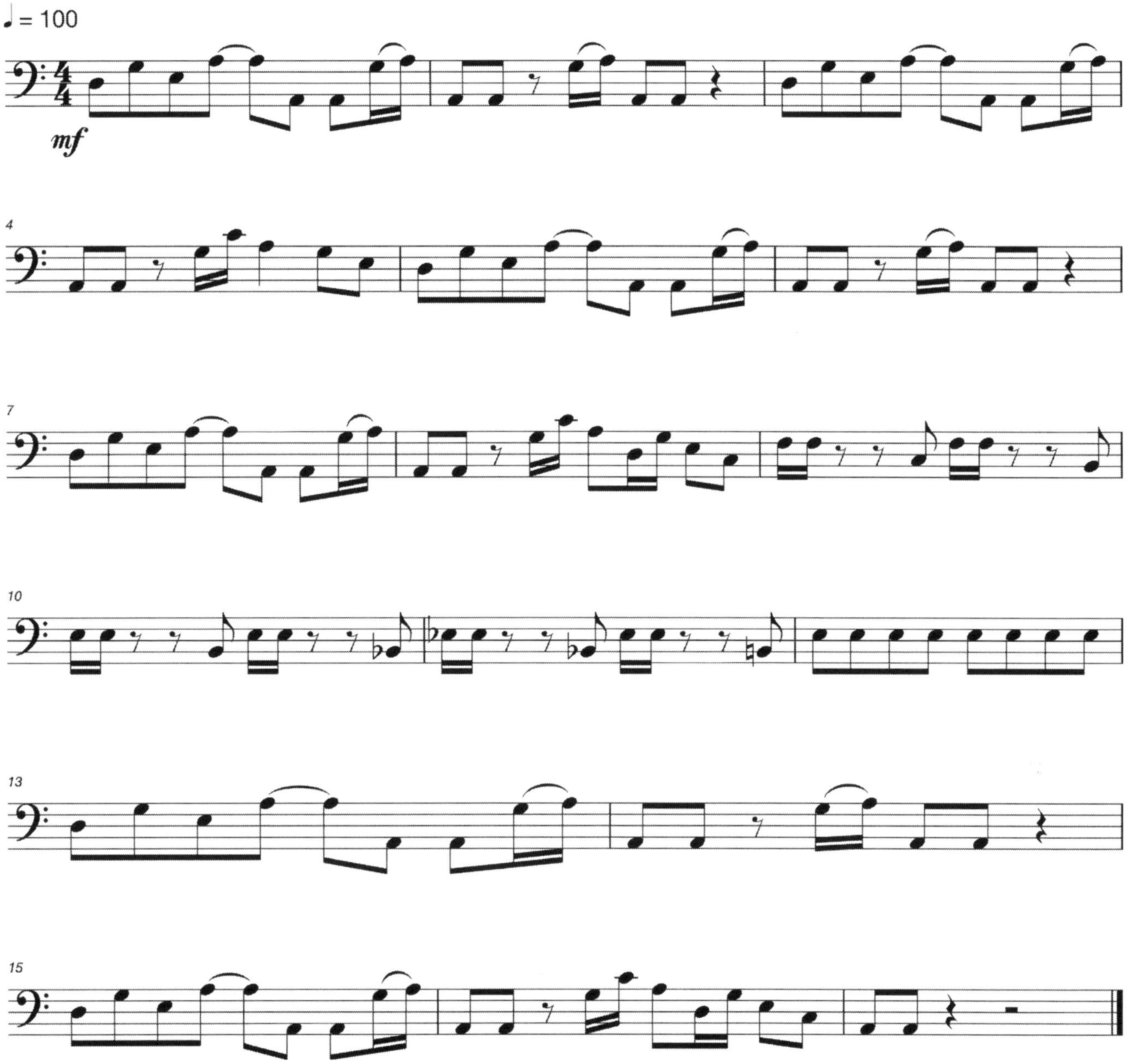

♩ = 100

mf

EXERCISE 70

This exercise is a rock bassline that features some obvious fourths movement in the first two bars. The middle section (bars 9-12) features a line that moves from the root note to the fourth. This fourth then drops down to the third of the implied chord. This is a common use of the fourth interval.

♩ = 100

mf

Chapter 7

Triplets

This chapter introduces a new rhythm, one that is unlike any of those that have been covered so far. That rhythm is the triplet.

So far, we have subdivided beats equally into either two or four and all of the rhythms covered up to this point have been based on these subdivisions. However, any rhythmic value can also be divided equally into three – doing so creates a **triplet**. Notes in a triplet are either bracketed or beamed together, with a number 3 written above them to show that the rhythmic division is not one that occurs naturally within the time signature.

Eighth Note Triplets

The first triplets that will be covered here are **eighth note triplets**. These are created by dividing one quarter note beat equally into three instead of two. When playing eighth note triplets it is important that all notes are played with equal duration. A good vocalisation for an eighth note triplet is the word 'diddly':

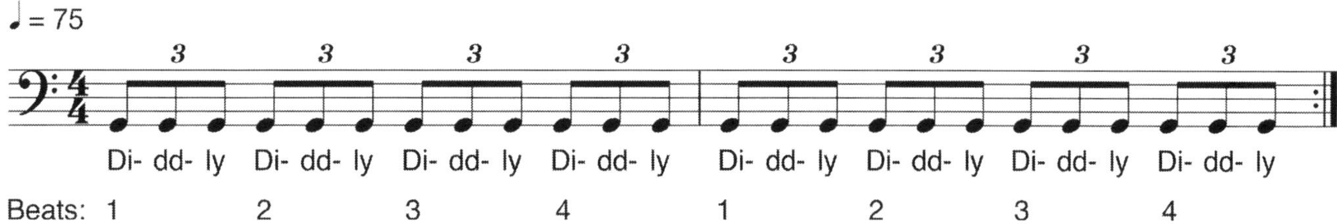

Obviously, any note of a triplet can also be a rest.

Quarter Note Triplets

Quarter note triplets are created by dividing a half note equally into three. As quarter notes are not beamed together, a quarter note triplet is written with a bracket above or below the notes:

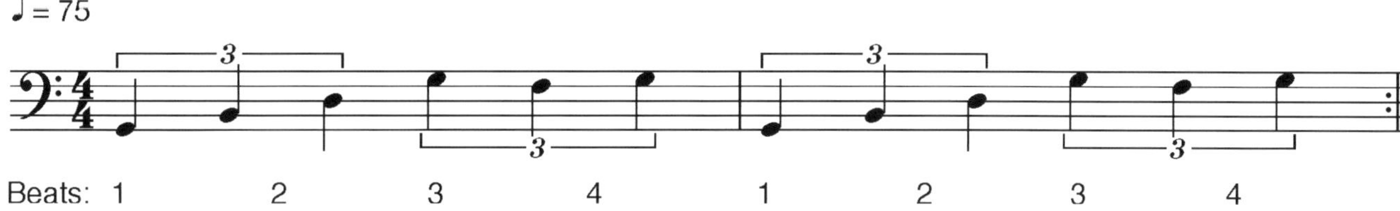

As they cover two full beats it is difficult to use a vocalisation for quarter note triplets. It's better to hear examples of them in use. With that in mind, be sure to listen closely to the accompanying audio files.

Half Note Triplets

Half note triplets are far less common than quarter or eighth note triplets and are the result of dividing a whole note into three. Again, these are written with a bracket over the notes:

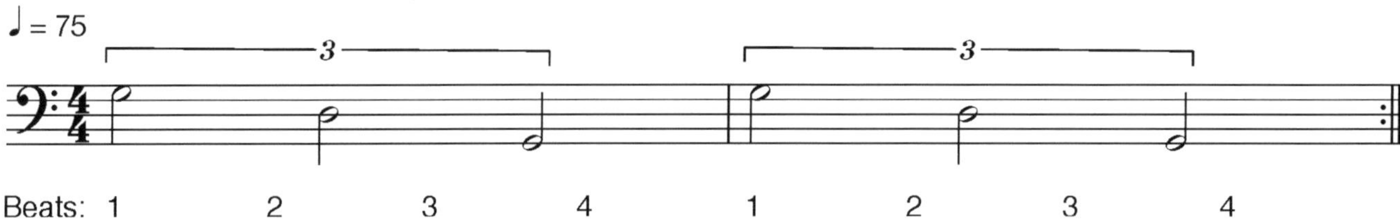

Sixteenth Note Triplets

Finally, an eighth note can be split into three, creating a **sixteenth note triplet**. This results in a very fast rhythm:

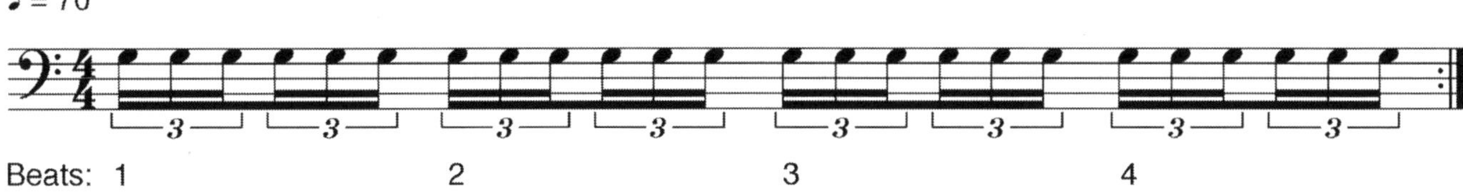

Rhythm Exercises

The next ten exercises are rhythm-only exercises that will allow you to work on playing these triplet rhythms without being distracted by pitches. Other rhythms from throughout this book and the previous one have been included here as well.

EXERCISE 71

EXERCISE 72

EXERCISE 73

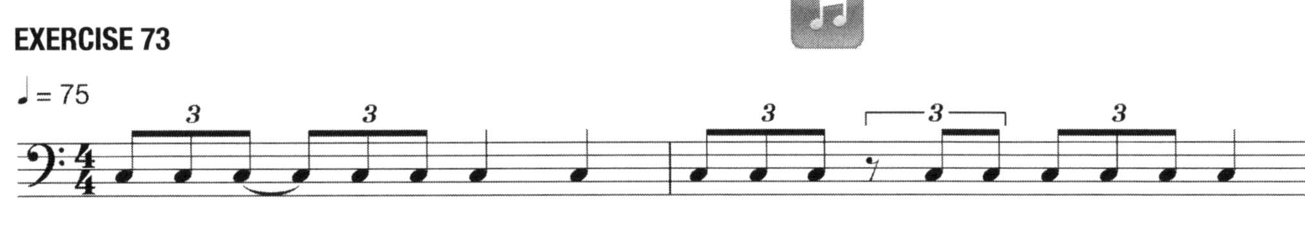

EXERCISE 74

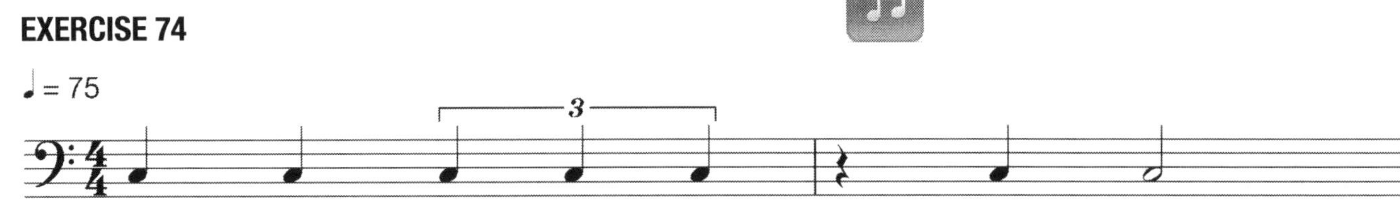

EXERCISE 75

EXERCISE 76
♩ = 75
3
EXERCISE 77
♩ = 75
3
EXERCISE 78
♩ = 75
3
EXERCISE 79
♩ = 75
3

EXERCISE 80

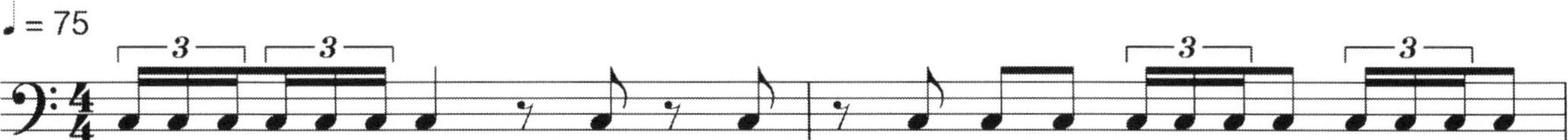

Chapter Summary

This chapter has introduced a new rhythmic concept: the triplet. As with all new rhythms, the best way to learn to read triplets is to listen to and study examples that use them. The following ten exercises will get you started with each of the triplet rhythms that were covered in this chapter.

EXERCISE 81

This is a basic eighth note triplet exercise that ascends and then descends the C major scale. Remember that an eighth note triplet works well with the vocalisation 'di-dd-ly'.

EXERCISE 82

This exercise uses eighth note triplets in the context of a riff. The tricky part of this exercise is accurately making the distinction between straight eighth note patterns, and triplet eighth note patterns – sometimes the two are used in close proximity. Listen carefully to the audio track when studying this exercise.

EXERCISE 83

This exercise is another riff that features eighth note triplets, although a rest is used on the first eighth note of some of the triplets. This pattern is repeated in most bars in order to reinforce the sound of this variation.

EXERCISE 84

This is another eighth note triplet exercise that includes rests. In this example, a rest has been used on the middle eighth note of the triplet. This pattern is then used for the majority of the line. You will hear that this creates a continuous, 'rolling triplet' feel in the music. This is known as a **shuffle**. The shuffle will be covered in more detail in the next chapter, which covers compound time signatures. These can be used as a clearer way of writing lines such as this.

EXERCISE 85

This is an exercise based on the diatonic arpeggios from the C major scale. It also makes extensive use of quarter note triplets – three notes evenly played in the space of two quarter notes. This exercise uses notes on some of the upper ledger lines that have not yet been covered. Look over these sections carefully and write the notes in with a pencil if you need to. Reading on ledger lines will be covered in Chapter 10.

EXERCISE 86

This exercise features the quarter note triplet in the context of a bassline.

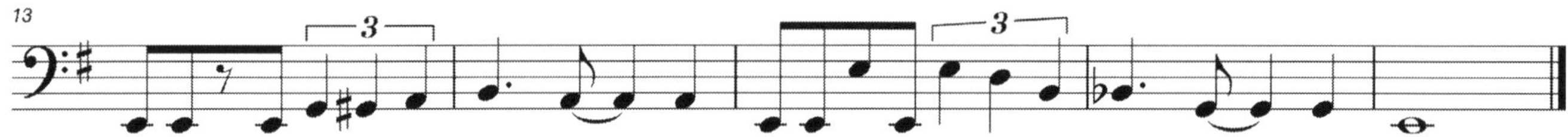

EXERCISE 87

Here's another exercise that uses the quarter note triplet. The opening bars are reminiscent of the bassline to 'Seven Nation Army' by The White Stripes, which is an excellent example of a quarter note triplet used in contemporary music.

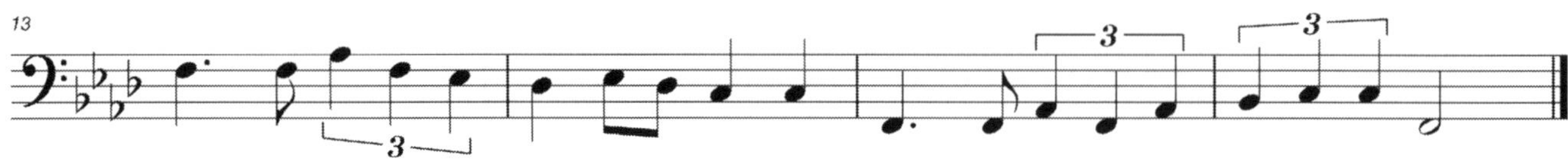

EXERCISE 88

This exercise uses half note triplets extensively. These are really tough to count accurately as they take place over a relatively long period of time – a bar. The best advice here is to listen closely to the audio file several times before attempting to play this line.

EXERCISE 89

This exercise features sixteenth note triplets, which as you will hear go by quite fast!

EXERCISE 90

This is another exercise that uses of sixteenth note triplets. This line is a groove in G minor that uses sixteenth note triplet figures extensively.

Chapter 8

Compound Time Signatures

This chapter covers 'compound' time signatures, which you will find are a little different to the 'simple' time signatures that have been used in the exercises so far. Compound time signatures allow music to be written with a different feel and therefore feature some rhythmic elements that might initially seem unusual. However, if you are comfortable with the triplet rhythms covered in the last chapter, compound time signatures shouldn't present too much of a problem.

Compound time signatures are different to simple time signatures because each beat is divided equally into three, rather than into two. This results in a triplet feel. Here's an example: if we compare 4/4 (a simple time signature) with 12/8 (the equivalent compound time signature) we can see that each one has **four beats in a bar**. The difference is that in 4/4 the beats are divided equally into two eighth notes, whereas in 12/8 the beats are divided equally into **three**:

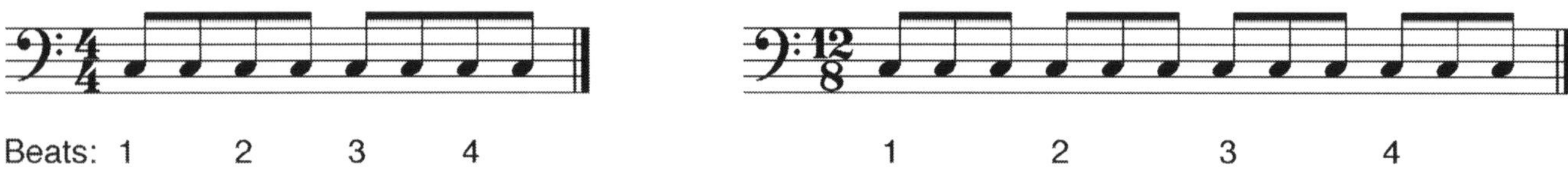

The difference between the two time signatures is hopefully obvious: whilst both have four beats to the bar, they each have a very different feel – 4/4 has a rigid, even feel, while 12/8 has a rolling, triplet feel. Whereas earlier in the book eighth note-based rhythms were counted as 1-*and*-2-*and*-3-*and*-4-*and*, 12/8 is counted as 1-*and*-*a*-2-*and*-*a*-3-*and*-*a*-4-*and*-*a*-. This emphasises the triplet feel and the four beats in the bar:

TIP!

The '8' in a compound time signature is not the beat unit, nor does the top number state the number of beats in a bar. In the case of a compound time signature, the beat unit is a dotted quarter note. To find out how many beats are in a bar, divide the top number of the time signature by three, i.e. 12/8 has four beats in a bar because 12 divided by 3 is 4.

Because an individual beat in 12/8 is equal to three eighth notes, a note lasting for a full beat must be written as a **dotted quarter note**, rather than just a quarter note. As you know, placing a dot after a note increases its rhythmic value by 50%:

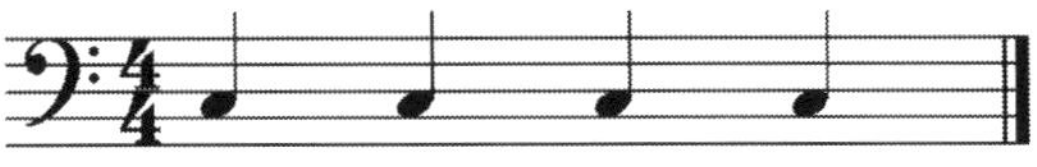

Beats: 1 2 3 4

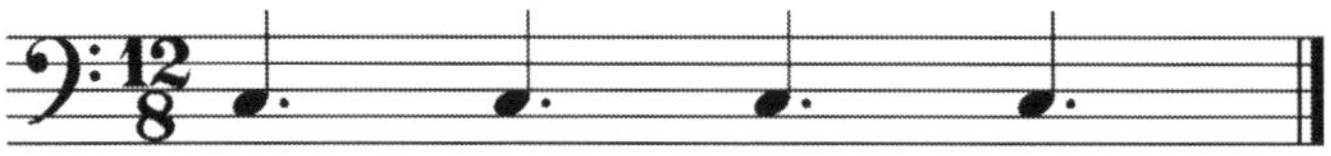

1 2 3 4

This applies to other note values as well – a note lasting for two full beats is now written as a dotted half note:

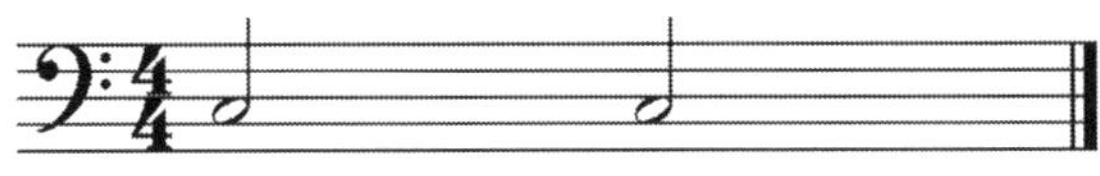

Beats: 1 2 3 4

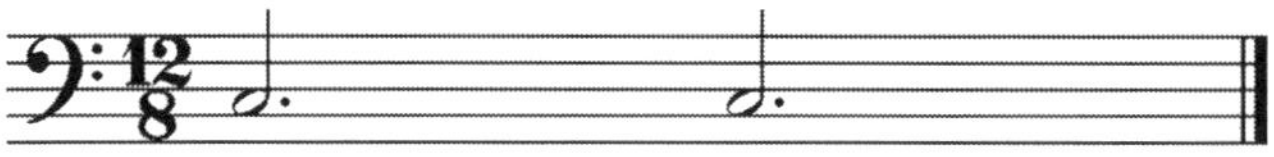

1 2 3 4

A note lasting for four whole beats is now written as a dotted whole note:

Beats: 1 2 3 4

1 2 3 4

For every simple time signature there is an equivalent compound time signature with the same number of beats in a bar. These are shown below:

Simple Time Signatures

Compound Time Signatures

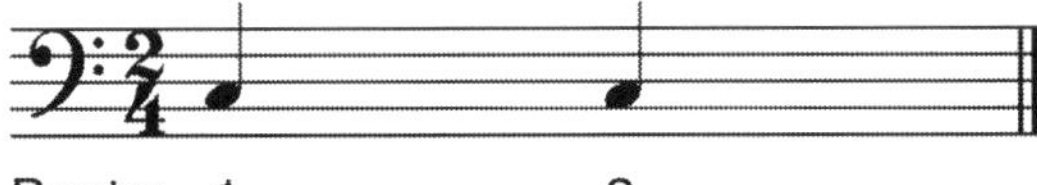

Beats: 1 2

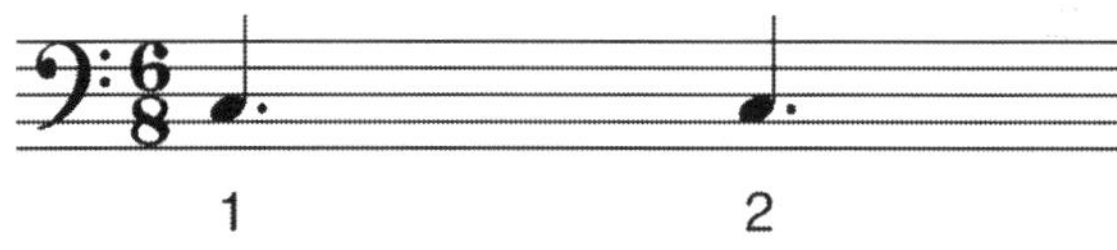

1 2

Beats: 1 2 3

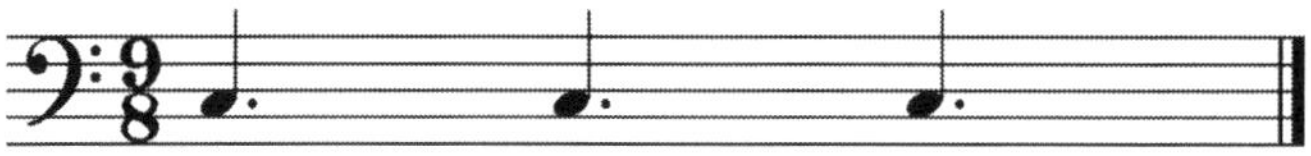

1 2 3

Beats: 1 2 3 4

1 2 3 4

This chapter will cover each of these compound time signatures and will illustrate how they are used. There are several exercises for each which will allow you the opportunity to put them to use in some real-world bass grooves.

12/8

12/8 time – which we have already discussed in some detail – is most often used as a more efficient way of writing a triplet-based 4/4 rhythm. Consider the following example:

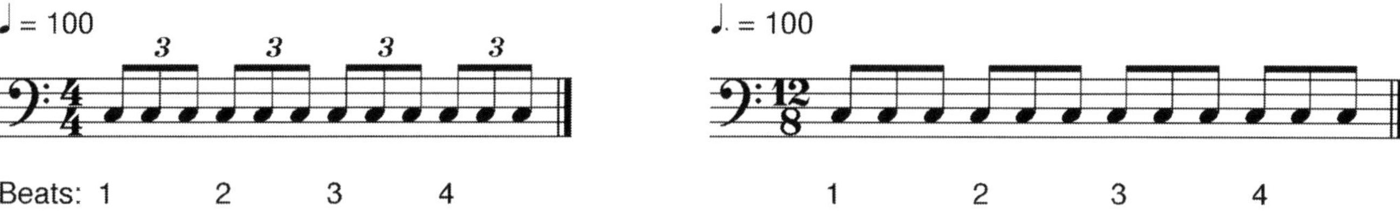

In the above example, the same bassline has been written out twice: first in 4/4, then in 12/8. As you can see, writing the line in 12/8 means that the number '3' does not need to be added over every beat to indicate a triplet. You will also notice that the metronome mark is different: in 4/4 it is written as a quarter note = 100bpm. In 12/8 it is written as a *dotted* quarter note = 100bpm.

TIP!

To see the difference it makes to write a triplet-based line using a compound time signature, refer back to Exercise 84 (Chapter 7). This exercise looks cluttered and unpleasant on the page due to all the triplets and would look much neater if it was written in 12/8.

12/8 time is commonly used to write music that has a **shuffle** rhythm, which is essentially a groove that is based on a triplet feel. This is also referred to as a **swing feel**. 12/8 is very often used in blues and jazz music but is also very common in other styles as well.

The following is a list of songs that are in 12/8. Have a listen to as many of these as you can in order to fully appreciate the feel of this time signature.

1. 'Sweet Home Chicago' – The Blues Brothers
2. 'Don't Stop' – Fleetwood Mac
3. 'Hoochie Coochie Man – Muddy Waters
4. 'The Lesson' – Victor Wooten
5. 'Lopsy Lu' – Stanley Clarke
6. 'Feeling Good' – Muse
7. 'Cry Me Out' – Pixie Lott
8. 'Oh Darling' – The Beatles
9. 'Misunderstanding' – Genesis
10. 'Hold the Line' – Toto

Hopefully by this point you have a good idea of how 12/8 time sounds. The following four exercises will allow you to practice reading in this new time signature.

EXERCISE 91

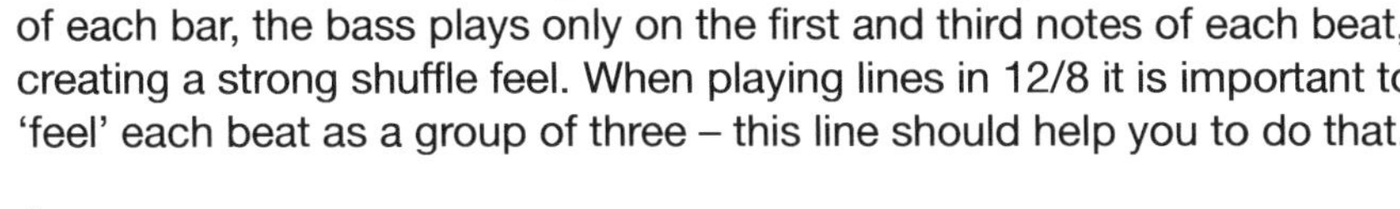

This exercise is a slow 12/8 groove over a blues progression. For most of each bar, the bass plays only on the first and third notes of each beat, creating a strong shuffle feel. When playing lines in 12/8 it is important to 'feel' each beat as a group of three – this line should help you to do that.

EXERCISE 92

This exercise is a blues bassline similar to Duck Dunn's part on The Blues Brothers classic 'Sweet Home Chicago'. Watch out for the quarter note-eighth note rhythm as seen at the beginning of the second bar: this means that the first note lasts for two thirds of the beat, with the second note falling on the last part. The effect is long-short, and helps reinforce the shuffle feel.

EXERCISE 93

This exercise is similar to Queen's 'Somebody to Love'.

♩. = 75

mf

4

7

10

13

15

EXERCISE 94

This exercise is similar to the slap groove that Stanley Clarke played on his classic track 'Lopsy Lu'. This is quite a complex exercise because of the use of ties, so listen carefully to the audio track and practice it slowly to begin with. You'll notice that ghost notes have been used in this exercise – these were covered back in Chapter 3.

It's worth noting that a 12/8 feel – or shuffle/swing feel – is sometimes indicated as part of the metronome mark. In instances such as these, the music would be written in 4/4, but an indication would be given that it should be swung, or played as a shuffle. This is sometimes done just by adding the words 'shuffle feel', or 'swing feel' to the metronome mark, but is often done using the following direction:

♫ = ♩ ♪ (3)

This tells the reader to interpret two eighth notes as triplet eighth notes:

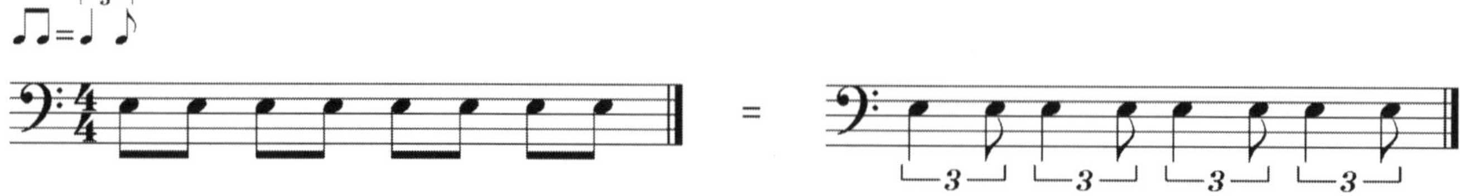

6/8

6/8 is the compound time equivalent of 2/4. As it is essentially the same thing as half of a bar of 12/8 it is often difficult to distinguish between songs written in 6/8 and those written in 12/8. Usually the phrasing of the melody, or the chord progression will suggest that 6/8 should be used instead of 12/8. Here are a selection of songs in 6/8 for you to listen to:

1. 'Nothing Else Matters' – Metallica
2. 'All Blues' – Miles Davis
3. 'Breaking the Girl' – Red Hot Chili Peppers
4. 'Everybody Hurts' – REM
5. 'Orion' – Metallica (middle section)

The following exercises will demonstrate how 6/8 is often used in contemporary music.

EXERCISE 95

This is a slow ballad in 6/8.

♩. = 70

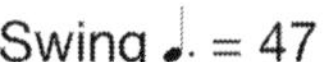

EXERCISE 96

This is a busier exercise and is similar to the use of 6/8 in the Red Hot Chili Peppers song 'Breaking the Girl'. Note that some of the eighth notes in each beat have been subdivided into sixteenth notes here and that the entire exercise is played with a swing feel. This means that the sixteenth notes that occur in the middle of some of the beats will be played as 'long-short'. Refer to the audio for guidance when learning this line.

EXERCISE 97

This exercise is similar to Cliff Burton's bassline during the middle section of the Metallica classic 'Orion'. This exercise might look quite complex, but the tempo is very slow.

EXERCISE 98

This exercise is a bassline for a variation on the blues progression.

9/8

9/8 is the final compound time signature and is by far the least common. It is the compound equivalent of 3/4 and is often used for waltzes that have a triplet feel. Here are some good examples of 9/8 being used in this way:

1. 'I Never Loved a Man (The Way I Love You)' by Aretha Franklin,
2. 'Jesu, Joy of Mans Desiring' by J.S.Bach,
3. 'Morning Has Broken' – Traditional

The following exercises demonstrate 9/8 in use.

EXERCISE 99

This is a simple ballad-style bassline that is similar to the feel of Aretha Franklin's 'I Never Loved a Man (The Way I Love You)'.

EXERCISE 100

This exercise features a bassline which really accentuates the triplet feel as well as highlighting the three beats in the bar.

Chapter 9
Sixths

By now you'll be aware of the benefits of being able to easily recognise and play the diatonic intervals on the bass. This chapter continues on from the previous interval chapters, this time covering the interval of the sixth. This is the widest interval that has been covered so far (aside from the octave) and is not quite so easy to recognise as some of the others.

Hopefully you will remember that the interval of a fifth is quite simple to spot: if the root note is on a line, then the fifth above will be two lines above. Similarly, if the root note is in a space, the fifth will be two spaces above. The interval of a sixth is one step wider than a fifth. Two examples are shown below:

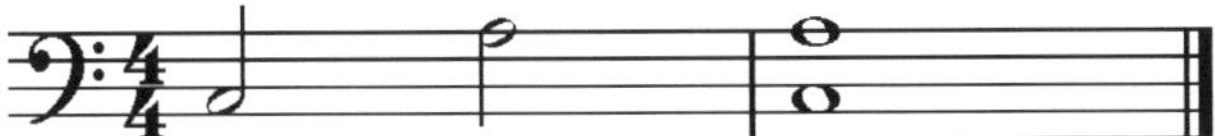

Sixth with root in a space

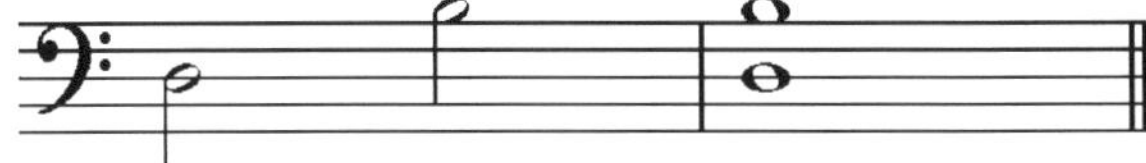

Sixth with root on a line

As in previous chapters, the second bar of each example above shows the notes stacked vertically in order to illustrate their appearance on the stave more clearly.

Like many other intervals, sixths come in two varieties – the **major sixth** and the **minor sixth**. A major sixth is separated by nine half steps:

C	C♯	D	D♯	E	F	F♯	G	G♯	A
	1	2	3	4	5	6	7	8	9

A minor sixth is separated by eight half steps:

C	C♯	D	D♯	E	F	F♯	G	A♭
	1	2	3	4	5	6	7	8

Whether the sixth in question is a major or minor sixth will depend on the key you are in, so when studying the exercises, remember to look at the key signature. Below are two examples:

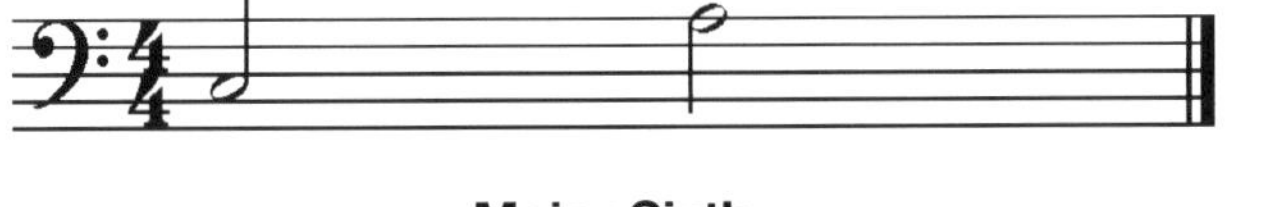

Major Sixth

Minor Sixth

In the first example the interval is a major sixth as C and A are separated by nine half steps. In the second, the interval is a minor sixth, as B and G are separated by eight half steps.

TIP!

For more information on sixths (or any other interval for that matter), be sure to check out Chapters 8 & 9 of *The Bass Guitarist's Guide to Scales & Modes*, also available from Bassline Publishing.

Playing sixths is much easier if you are familiar with the common fretboard positions for each type. These are illustrated below:

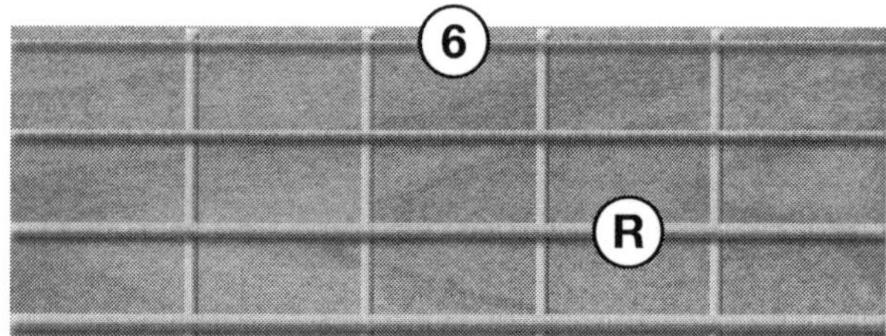

Major Sixth

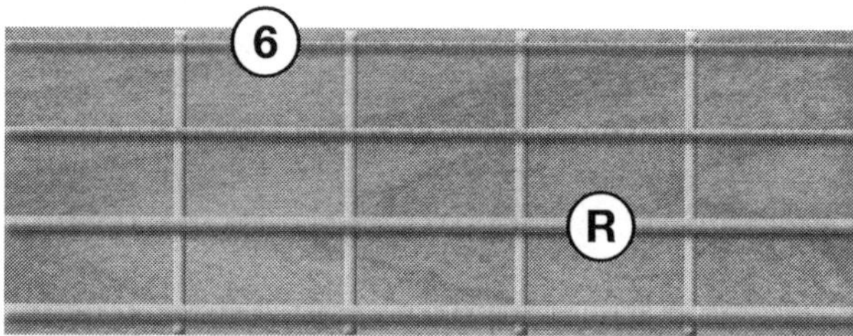

Minor Sixth

As you can see, the major sixth is two strings away and one fret back, whilst the minor sixth is two strings away and two frets back.

Chapter Summary

This chapter has focused on the widest interval covered so far, the sixth. This interval is not as easy to recognise on the stave as more symmetrical intervals such as thirds and fifths, so you will probably find that the ability to spot these quickly takes longer to develop. The following ten exercises will get you started on putting sixths to use in some basslines.

EXERCISE 101

This exercise is a bassline that works over a repeating two bar chord progression: D and C in the first bar, then G in the second bar. In the first bar the bass plays the third of the chord, followed by the root note, which is a sixth higher. This is quite a common move for a bass player and outlines the sound of the chord without focusing too heavily on the root note. Watch out for the tricky fill in bar 8 – the last note of bar 7 is part of this fill, which consists of an ascending minor sixth from the B to the G, a descending major sixth from the F♯ down to the A, and another descending major sixth from the E down to the low G. In bar 9 the bass plays the fifth of the chord followed by the third, which is a major sixth above. No root notes are played here, but the sound of the overall chord is still obvious.

EXERCISE 102

This exercise is a funk groove that uses an idea commonly used in funk tunes – root, sixth, minor seventh. This motif is used at the beginning of each two-bar phrase. The second bar of each phrase is a series of different fills that use sixths.

EXERCISE 103

This exercise looks rather unpleasant on paper but features a lot of repetition. The opening sixth figures are simpler to play if you finger the F♯ and G♯ at the ninth and eleventh frets of the A-string, then play the high E on the G-string. This figure is then repeated two frets down on the next beat of the bar. All of the sixths in this line can be played in this way.

♩ = 90

mf

EXERCISE 104

This is a slower exercise that is based on a root – sixth – fifth movement. In bars 5-8 the opening idea is developed and another sixth is played above the fifth.

TIP!

You will see a small 'o' written beneath some of the notes in this exercise. This symbol is used to indicate that an open string is the easiest way to perform the note. In this bassline the symbol is written beneath most of the low A notes indicating that the open A-string would be the best place to play them.

EXERCISE 105

This exercise is a typical soul bassline and is similar to the groove on the Eddie Floyd classic 'Knock on Wood'.

EXERCISE 106

This exercise has a slow tempo and is based on a sixteenth note feel.

EXERCISE 107

This exercise features some sixths played in the upper register of the bass. Under many of these you will see the performance direction 'let ring', which means that you should allow the notes to ring together for a chordal effect. For example, in the first bar, the F♯ should be allowed to continue ringing whilst the A below is played. As you will hear, the chordal effect of this interval sounds very effective on the bass.

EXERCISE 108

This is a classic rock bassline that makes extensive use of sixths.

♩ = 100

5

9

let ring

13

EXERCISE 109

This is a heavier rock riff that uses sixths.

♩ = 100

5

9

EXERCISE 110

This exercise has a sixth at the beginning of each two-bar phrase and is another example of a line that starts with an **anacrusis**.

Chapter 10

Ledger Lines

Ledger lines were first mentioned in Chapter 3 of the *Beginner Level* book and as you probably know, are the additional lines that are used to accommodate notes that occur above or below the stave. Although you will have had the opportunity to read some notes on ledger lines in some of the exercises earlier in the book, this chapter focuses on them in more detail.

The illustration below shows the notes on ledger lines above the stave, and their locations on the bass:

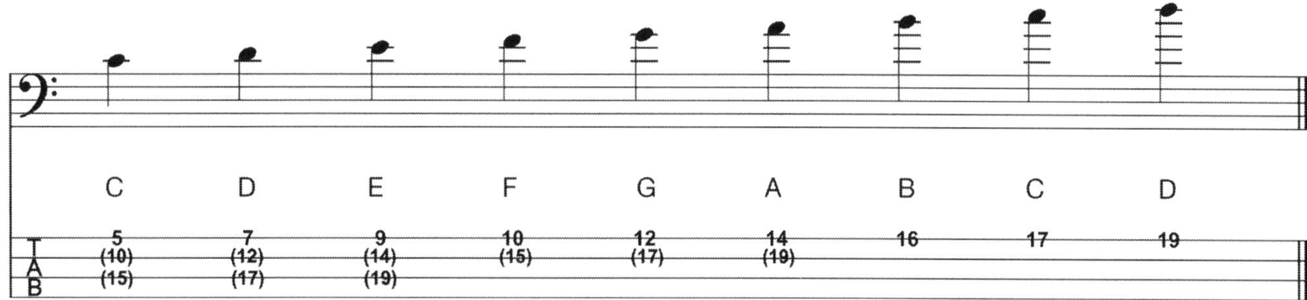

There are of course notes that exist *below* the bass stave as well, and in fact the first of these is the low E on a conventional 4-string bass. Notes lower than this will be discussed in the next book in this series, which will cover reading music on a 5-string bass, an instrument that allows access to notes lower than E.

Octave Higher and Lower Symbols

Although they will be not be used in the exercises in this chapter, it's a good idea for you to be aware of some notation conventions that can be used in place of writing notes on ledger lines. Consider the following example:

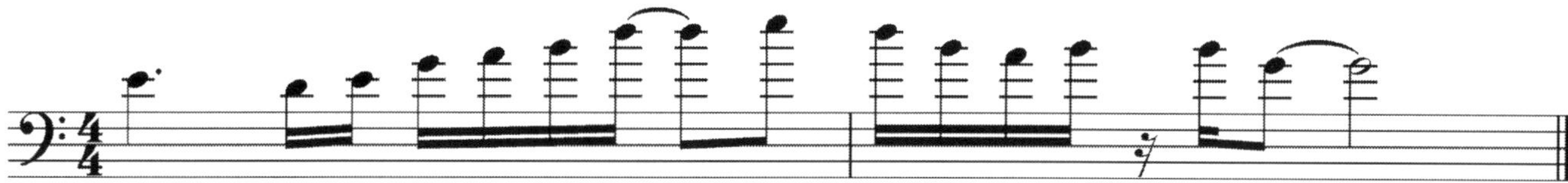

As you can see, the entirety of this passage of notes is written on ledger lines and is therefore quite challenging to read. In situations such as this, it is common to write the notes an octave lower and use the '8va' direction to indicate that they should be played an octave higher:

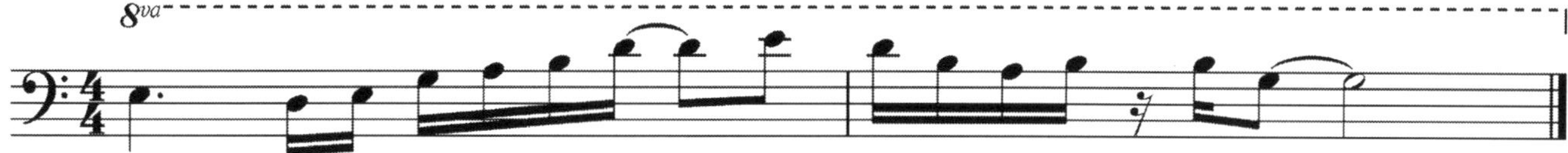

Similarly, if a composer wished a passage of music to be played an octave lower than where it was written, the '8vb' direction would be written below the notes, again accompanied by a dashed horizontal line.

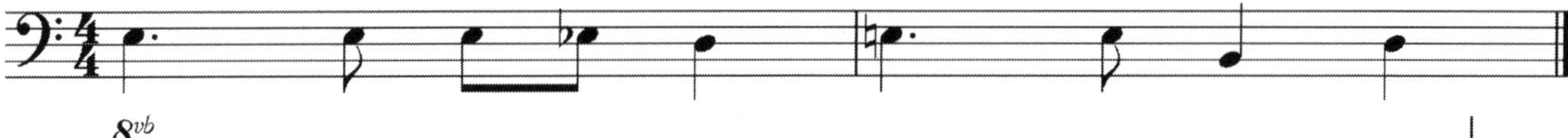

This would be played an octave lower than where it is written, although to do so would require a 5-string bass:

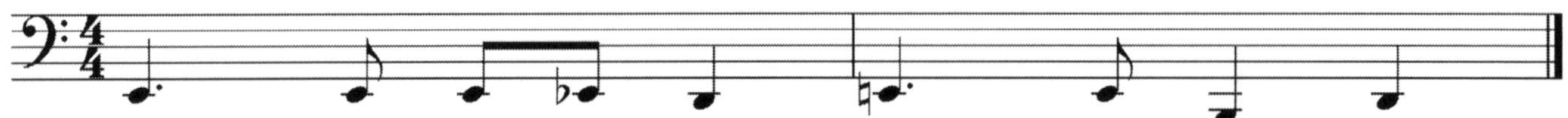

Chapter Summary

There is little else to discuss with regard to ledger lines. You should study the illustration on the previous page and become as familiar as you can with the location of the notes written on the ledger lines. Although they are not used in every bassline, there will be instances where you will be required to read music in this register, and you should be comfortable doing so.

EXERCISE 111

This exercise is in E minor and each bar begins with two low E's, clearly establishing the tonality. These are followed by simple upper register melody lines.

EXERCISE 112

This exercise is in the key of F minor and includes some very high notes. There are also some difficult rhythms, so you might want to play (or clap) through the line first just using one note in order to focus on the rhythm. Remember to look out for obvious intervals – for example the first and third bars start with the interval of a perfect fifth.

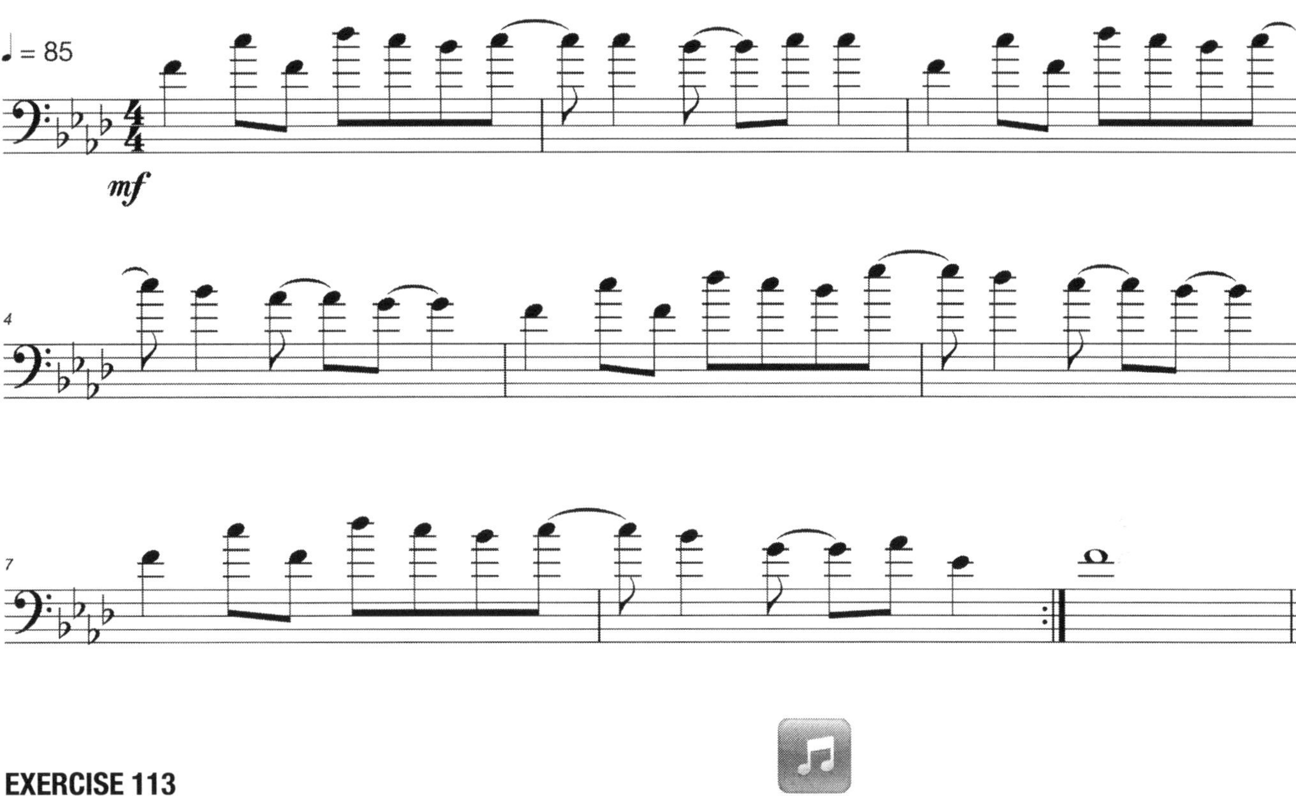

EXERCISE 113

This exercise looks complicated, but there is a lot of rhythmic repetition. Once you have cracked the first two bars, you will see there is almost no variation in the rhythms at all.

EXERCISE 114

This exercise is in 3/4 time and has a quick tempo – obviously you should study this in free time, or at a much slower tempo until you are able to read the notes accurately. The performance direction 'let ring' is used here. The A at the beginning of each bar should be played as the open A-string and allowed to continue ringing whilst the upper notes are played. This creates a chordal effect which is very effective on the bass.

EXERCISE 115

This exercise is based on the harmonic minor scale, one that creates some very unique sounds. The 'let ring' direction is used again here to reinforce the chordal nature of the line.

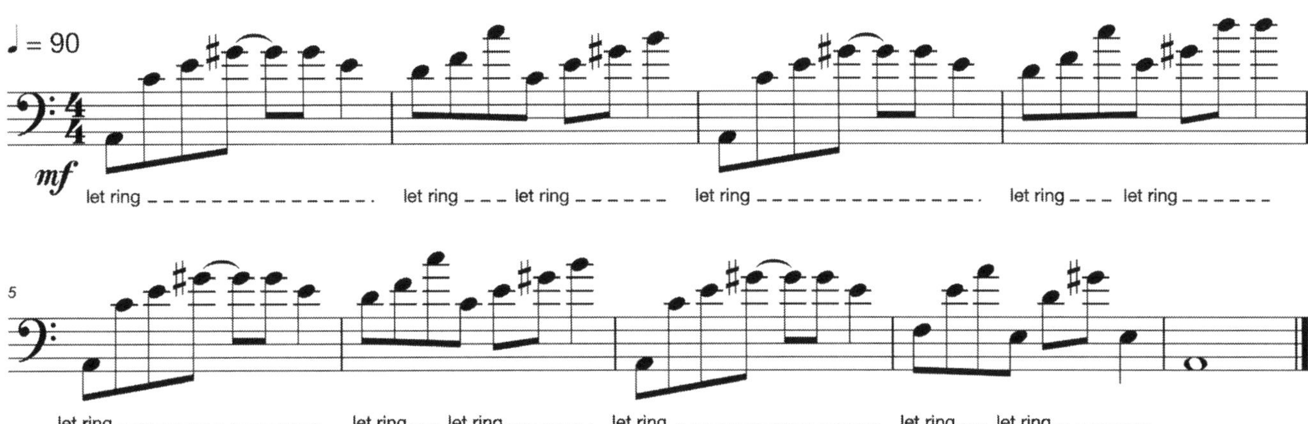

TIP!

For more information on the harmonic minor scale, be sure to check out *The Bass Guitarist's Guide to Scales & Modes*, which is also available from Bassline Publishing.

Intermediate Level

Exercise Area

This final section brings together all of the elements that have been covered in this book, including compound time signatures, sixteenth note grooves, triplets, dynamics and reading on ledger lines above the stave. These longer exercises will allow you to get your teeth into some challenging 'real-world' basslines and will certainly put the skills you have acquired so far to the test.

If you have successfully played through all of the exercises in this book, you should find nothing in this set of exercises that is unfamiliar to you. This is not to say that you'll find them easy – far from it! These are very challenging lines and will require patient study. Remember that you are not expected to sight read any of the exercises here – the intention is that you study them and learn to play them slowly, correcting mistakes as you go. Once you have learnt them, keep playing them (along with all of the other exercises in the book), over and over, always following the music as you play. Doing so will help to reinforce the connections in your brain between what you are seeing and what you are playing.

The following ten basslines have been recorded with full backing tracks in order to give you the chance to play lines in different styles with a backing band. As before, two audio tracks are available for each exercise, one with recorded bass and one without.

Finally, it's a great idea to refresh your memory on the four key points to be aware of before studying any piece of music:

1. What key is the piece in? Remember that the key signature can relate to either a major key, or its relative minor.
2. What is the time signature? Usually this will be 4/4, but not always. You should also look at the tempo at the beginning of the piece as well. Faster tempos are usually more challenging.
3. Are there any navigation marks? Look out for repeat marks or Coda directions, and make sure you understand where they go.
4. Are there any particularly difficult parts? Look out for sections that look challenging. It's a good idea to go over any rhythms you find difficult or pitches you can't remember before you start working on the exercise.

Good luck with these exercises. There are some very challenging lines here that will require a lot of time and patience in order to master them.

EXERCISE 116

This exercise is written in 6/8 time, a compound time signature. Remember that in 6/8, there are two beats in each bar, and each is divided equally into three eighth notes.

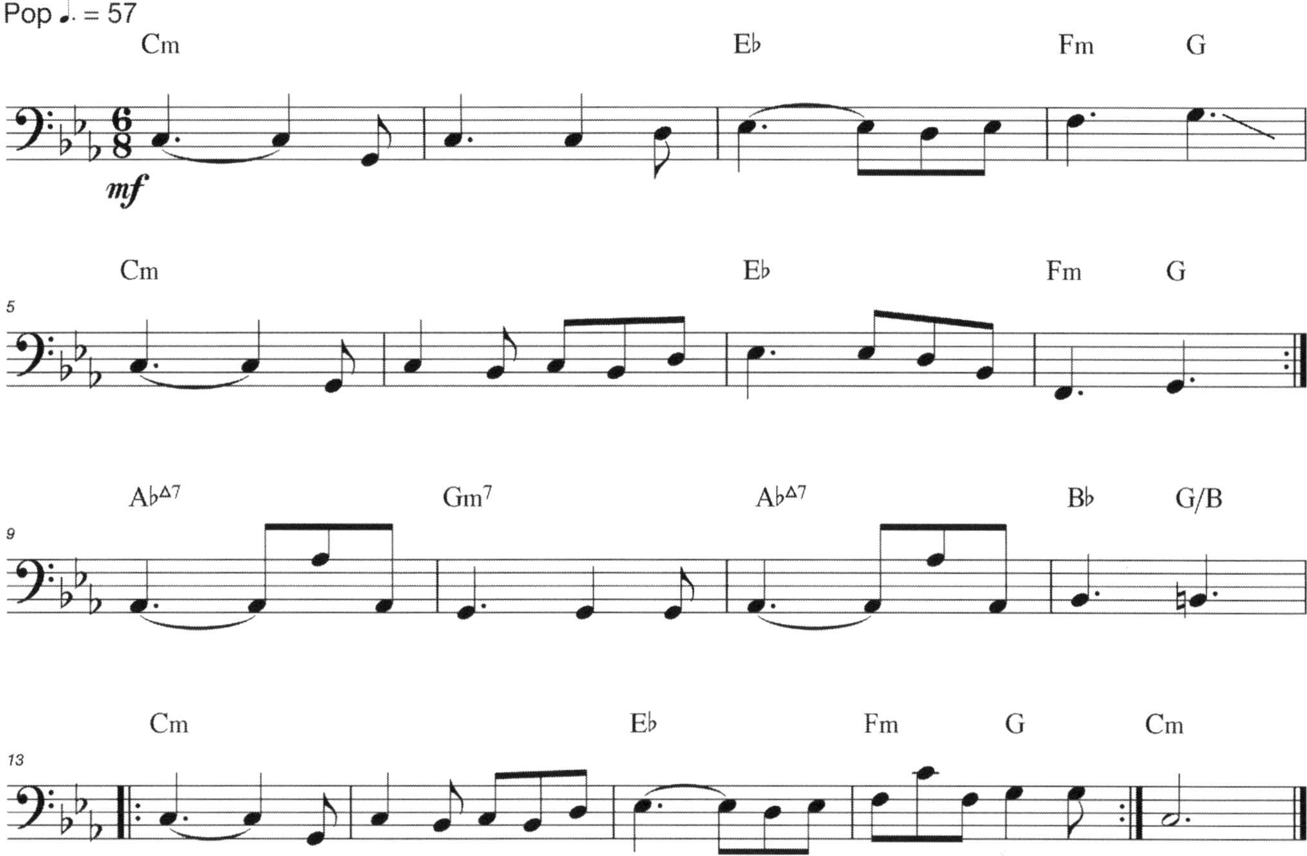

EXERCISE 117

This exercise is a real tip of the hat to Rage Against the Machine and will probably look terrifying to you initially! Hopefully after a few minutes of study you will notice that the tempo is quite slow and there is a lot of repetition. This is predominantly an exercise for you to use to practice reading continuous sixteenth notes, but there are also some triplet figures here as well. Once you've learnt the various parts, you should concentrate on following the various dynamics that are written.

Rock ♩ = 85

N.C.

EXERCISE 118

This exercise uses another compound time signature, this time 12/8. In 12/8 time there are four beats to the bar, but each one divides naturally into three eighth notes rather than two. This is a rock shuffle with a quick tempo, but you should find that it is a lot easier to play than it might look.

Rock Shuffle ♩. = 145

Am

f

F G F

4

Em Am

8

F D G

11

F D G Am

15

Am

19

EXERCISE 119

This long exercise will keep you busy for a while. This is a pop/rock track that features a very active bassline. Although there are no sixteenth note rhythms to worry about, there are a lot of melodic eighth note lines, many of which will require some thought in terms of fingerings and position playing. The piece also starts with an **anacrusis**, a pick-up phrase that is less than a bar in length. As you'll hear on the recording, this phrase, consisting of three eighth notes, starts on the 'and' of beat three. The last note is tied into the first main bar of the piece. You'll notice that this idea is used repeatedly throughout. There are also some dynamics to watch out for in this piece. Take your time with this one, there is a lot of information to digest here.

Pop Rock ♩ = 115

G Am C D G Am C D G

mf

5 Am Em D Am G

9 Am C D G Am C D Em

13 C Am D Am

17 F Em

20 G D C Am C Em

f

24 G D C Am F

continued...

28
C
G
Am
C
D
G
32
Am
C
D
Em
35
C
F
C
G

EXERCISE 120

This exercise is a very challenging funk bassline that uses many of the sixteenth note rhythms that were covered in Chapters 1 and 5. Sixteenth notes are by far the toughest thing to read for a bass player, so don't be concerned if you find this line particularly difficult – remember that you are not expected to sight read it.

The opening figure of this line is an upper register phrase. It is recommended that you play the first two notes (D and G) at the nineteenth and seventeenth frets of the G and D-strings respectively. There is then a slide downwards, then the next two notes should be played at the twelfth and tenth frets of the G and D-strings. An open string symbol has been used above the D on the third beat to indicate that the open D-string is the best place to play this note. The second bar of this phrase is much simpler. Once you have learnt the two first two bars of this piece you will have conquered the hardest part!

Funk ♩ = 90

Am7

F△9 E7(♯9)

N.C.

1.

2.

F△9 E7(♯9)

Am7

F△9 E7(♯9) Am7

EXERCISE 121

This is a rock groove that is much simpler than it looks on paper. Although the opening bars are busy, you should quickly notice that the three-note phrase on the first beat of each bar is repeated on the second and third beats. There are some tasty blues and pentatonic licks in bars 4 and 8.

Rock ♩ = 95

N.C. B♭5 N.C. C5 B♭5 N.C. B♭5

4 N.C. C5 N.C. C5 D5

7 N.C. B♭5 N.C. F5 E♭5

10 N.C. F5 E♭5 N.C.

13 B♭5 N.C. C5 B♭5

15 N.C. C5 N.C. G5

TIP!

For more information on the blues and pentatonic scales, be sure to check out *The Bass Guitarist's Guide to Scales & Modes*, also available from Bassline Publishing.

EXERCISE 122

This exercise is a melodic bassline over a repeating one-bar chord progression that is played with a reggae groove. There are some triplet figures to watch out for here, particularly at the end of the piece. The final note is delayed here and falls on the 'and' of the first beat of the next bar. Count this carefully.

EXERCISE 123

This is another challenging funk bassline. Although this is a tough exercise, it is another in which you will find that there is a certain amount of repetition. After you have learnt the first few bars, you will find that many of the other bars are either repeats, or variations on them. There are also quite a lot of dynamics written in this piece – staccato dots for example – so be sure to pay close attention to these in order to play the line as it is intended.

Funk ♩ = 105

Gm7 Bb C

mf

3 Gm7 Bb C

5 Gm7 Bb C

7 Gm7 Bb C

9 Eb∆7 Cm7 Eb∆7 F F#o

13 Gm7 Bb C

15 Gm7 Bb C Gm7

EXERCISE 124

This exercise is a heavy rock riff that features quarter note triplets and sixteenth note lines. After you have mastered the first two bars you will once again find that most of the other bars are merely variations on the same idea. The middle section is a descending sixteenth note line. The challenging part of this line is that the note changes on the last subdivision of the second and fourth beats and is then tied into the next beat. This will be hard to read initially, but once you can play it, it should seem very logical.

Heavy Rock ♩ = 85

N.C. A5 N.C.

4 A5 N.C. A5 G5 N.C.

7 A5 B5 E5 D5 A/C♯

10 C5 G/B E5 D5 A/C♯

12 C5 G/B N.C. A5 G5 N.C.

15 N.C. A5 N.C. E5

EXERCISE 125

This final piece is the bassline for a ballad, which uses a common set of jazz chord changes. The tempo is very slow here, so even the occasional sixteenth note phrases will be quite simple to play. Dynamics – such as slides – are very important here.

A Ballad ♩ = 60

B♭Δ7 Fm7 B♭7 E♭Δ7 E♭m7 A♭7

mp

5 B♭Δ7 Gm7 Cm7 F7 Dm7 G7 Cm7 F7

A

9 B♭Δ7 Fm7 B♭7 E♭Δ7 E♭m7 A♭7

13 B♭Δ7 Gm7 Cm7 F7 B♭6

B

17 Fm7 B♭7♭9 E♭Δ7

21 Em7 A7 C7 Dm7♭5 G7♭9 Cm7 F7

let ring – – – let ring – – –

A

25 B♭Δ7 Fm7 B♭7 E♭Δ7 E♭m7 A♭7

29 B♭Δ7 Gm7 Cm7 F7 B♭6 Cm7 F7 B♭Δ7